BLOOD OF THE MARTYRS, SEED OF THE CHURCH

BLOOD
OF THE
MARTYRS
Stories of Catholics
Who Died
for Their Faith

SEED
OF THE
CHURCH

PAUL THIGPEN

CHARIS

SERVANT PUBLICATIONS
ANN ARBOR, MICHIGAN

Charis Books is an imprint of Servant Publications especially designed to serve
Roman Catholics.

All Scripture quotations, unless otherwise indicated, are taken from the Revised
Standard Version of the Bible, copyrighted 1946, 1952, 1971 by the Division of
Christian Education of the National Council of Churches of Christ in the USA.
Used by permission.

Published by Servant Publications
P.O. Box 8617
Ann Arbor, Michigan 48107

Cover design by Eric Walljasper

01 02 03 10 9 8 7 6 5 4 3 2 1

Printed in the United States of America
ISBN 0-56955-215-0

LIBRARY OF CONGRESS CATALOGING-IN-PUBLICATION DATA

Thigpen, Thomas Paul, 1954-
    Blood of the martyrs, seed of the church: stories of Catholics who died for their
faith / Paul Thigpen.
        p. cm.
    Includes bibliographical references.
    ISBN 1-56955-215-0 (alk. paper)
    1. Christian martyrs—Biography. I. Title.

BX4655.3 T48 2001
272'.092'2—dc21
[B}
                                                                    00-065918

For my dear friends

Chuck and Liesa,

who, like the martyrs,

have taught me so much about

sacrifice, courage, and commitment.

Contents

"THE BLOOD OF CHRISTIANS IS SEED" 9
An Introduction

1. "AN IMAGE OF HIS MASTER" 15
Christ, the Model of Martyrdom

2. "CRYING IN THE WILDERNESS" 33
The Forerunner of Christ's Passion
    St. John the Baptist

3. "THE CUP THAT I DRINK, YOU WILL DRINK" ...47
Martyrs of the First Generation
    St. Stephen 56
    St. James, the Brother of John 61
    The Other Apostles 63
    St. Paul 66
    St. Peter 72

4. "WE MUST OBEY GOD RATHER THAN MEN" 75
Martyrs Executed by the State
    St. Polycarp of Smyrna 81
    St. Perpetua 89
    Perfectus 102
    Isaac and Others 103
    Flora and Maria 105
    Eulogius and Leocritia 106
    St. Pelagius 107

5. "THE OVERTHROWER OF OUR GODS"..............111
   Martyrs of the Mission Fields
      St. Justin the Philosopher *112*
      St. Boniface *118*
      Blessed Michael Nakashima *129*
      St. Isaac Jogues..*132*
      The Martyrs of Uganda *138*

6. "MY GREATEST ENEMIES, MY BEST FRIENDS" 143
   Martyrs Killed by Other Christians
      St. Flavian of Constantinople........................*145*
      St. Thomas à Becket *149*
      St. Thomas More *156*
      St. Andrew Bobola...*161*

7. "LONG LIVE CHRIST THE KING!" 165
   Martyrs of the Twentieth Century
      Blessed Miguel Pro...*167*
      St. Teresa Benedicta (Edith Stein) *179*
      Servant of God Marcel Van *190*

8. "IN PERSECUTION THE CHURCH BEGINS 195
   AND ENDS"
   The Triumph of the Martyrs

Notes..*207*

"THE BLOOD OF CHRISTIANS IS SEED"
An Introduction

Truly, truly, I say to you, unless a grain of wheat falls into the earth and dies, it remains alone; but if it dies, it bears much fruit. He who loves his life loses it, and he who hates his life in this world will keep it for eternal life. If anyone serves me, he must follow me.

JOHN 12:24-26

We multiply whenever we are mown down by you; the blood of Christians is seed.

Tertullian, *Apology*, 50, 13

The morning sunrise, golden and bloody, splashed across the skies over Tybee Island, Georgia, where I often walk on the beach to pray. My mind turned to thoughts of another morning, long ago, just a short distance down the Georgia coast. It was there, a little over four hundred years ago, that Servant of God Pedro de Corpa—a Spanish Franciscan missionary priest—had died, his skull crushed by a tomahawk.

Juanillo, the baptized son of the local native chief, led the war party. His people, the Guales, were traditionally polygamists, so at baptism they had to promise to live in a permanent marriage with only one spouse, according to God's law. Nevertheless, Juanillo had chafed under that restriction, and he'd finally taken a second wife, scandalizing the other native converts.

Admonitions from the friars to keep his baptismal promises stirred the young prince to rage rather than repentance. After murdering Fr. Corpa, Juanillo placed the missionary's head on a pike at the mission landing, then forced the village women to engage in a perverse orgy, as if to boast of his newly regained sexual "freedom." A few days later he and his warriors sought out and killed four other friars in nearby missions.[1]

My thoughts on the beach then returned to the present, and to the recent news reports of an American priest murdered in Kenya—the third Catholic missionary to be assassinated in four years in that East African nation. For nearly four decades Fr. John Kaiser had labored there and spoken out publicly against human rights abuses by high-ranking officials. In retaliation for his latest protests against injustice, he had been killed by a gunshot wound in the back of the head.[2]

Like the poor, the martyrs, it seems, are always with us.

They are with us, indeed, not only in their deaths, but in their triumph as well. For like St. John the Baptist, who also was killed for calling powerful sinners to repentance, the sixteenth-century martyrs of Georgia and the twentieth-century martyrs of Kenya have by no means died in vain. Thousands came to know the Lamb of God because St. John had pointed the way to him. Within a century after Fr. Corpa's murder, in part because of his witness, tens of thousands of Native Americans in what is now the southeastern United States also came to love Jesus Christ. No doubt in the dawning years of the third millennium, the fruits of Fr. Kaiser's witness will multiply in Kenya and beyond to give Christ's hope and courage to the powerless.

This fertile, living, divine power is what the ancient Christian theologian Tertullian spoke about when he told the enemies of the Church: "The blood of Christians is seed." Because we need that power today more than ever, I offer this little collection of martyrs' stories, trusting that what these saints tell us by their deaths will change what we do with our lives. If we take to heart the truth to which they bear witness, we can share the hope of Pope John Paul II that their martyrdoms will provide "the foundation for a new world ... and a new civilization."[3]

One of an author's most difficult tasks—narrowing the subject matter to fit the space allowed—has created perplexing challenges in producing this book, because the story of every Christian martyr cries out to be told. I was guided in part by a desire to show the universality of martyrdom, hoping to include subjects from the widest possible variety of backgrounds and circumstances. Yet even then the decisions proved agonizing: How in the world, for example, do you choose between St. Thomas More and St. Edmund Campion? Between St. Agnes and St. Perpetua?

Ultimately, the most important questions that guided me were these: Whose stories do we need most to hear in our present spiritual, social, cultural, and political climate? Which martyrs will most unsettle us and shake us out of our easy assumptions about the Christian life? Doubtless my own special interests and blind spots will be reflected in the way I answered these questions, and every reader will find that I've left out some favorite saint. I therefore ask you to forgive me now, before you begin, and to focus instead on the gripping accounts of the men, women, and children who appear in these pages. Each one of them has profound lessons to teach us, if we will only listen.

This text is for a popular rather than a scholarly audience, as a glance at the endnotes will show. Nevertheless, those who wish to probe more deeply into the lives of the martyrs will find even in these meager citations plenty of further reading. I especially recommend Robert Royal's new *Catholic Martyrs of the Twentieth Century* (Crossroad, 2000); Joseph N. Tylenda's

Jesuit Saints and Martyrs (Loyola, 1998); and the multiple works of Ann Ball on Catholic saints and martyrs (several of which are cited in the notes).

I wish to thank Ann Ball for her help in researching the life of Blessed Miguel Pro. Thanks also to Marie Schoettle for providing information about the Franciscan martyrs of Georgia; I pray that their cause for canonization may soon find success.

As always, I'm grateful to Bert Ghezzi, Heidi Saxton, and all the wonderful folks at Servant who make it possible for a work such as this to become a reality.

A word about the use of the term "Catholic" with regard to the earliest saints: Some might consider it an anachronism to speak of "Catholic martyrs" when we include in this collection the first generation of Christians. It's true that we don't have any surviving record of the term "Catholic" being used to refer to the Church until St. Ignatius of Antioch's epistle to the Smyrneans, written sometime before his martyrdom in about the year A.D. 107. Yet this reference is indeed very early, and ancient tradition has it that St. Ignatius, whose earthly lifetime might well have overlapped that of our Lord, succeeded St. Peter or perhaps St. Peter's successor at Antioch.

The good bishop would thus have known personally the generation of the apostles, and when he spoke of the Church that Christ had founded through them, he spoke of it as the Catholic Church. I see no reason to argue with him, and many good reasons to imitate him. Whether or not they would have used the term for themselves, St. John the Baptist, St. Stephen, and the apostles are all foundation stones in the great two-thousand-year-old edifice of the Catholic Church; and that Church quite reasonably claims them as her own.

Finally, I should clarify that in this book I'm using the term "martyr" in a general sense to mean someone who died voluntarily for the sake of Christian faith or Christian morals. The Church uses the term "martyr" officially in a much more specific sense, designating someone whose death met certain conditions, as determined by a rather extensive and complicated examination process by Church officials entrusted with the task. Martyrs in this sense may be those who died for refusing to deny the Christian faith or to perform some act inconsistent with Christian faith or morals. They are typically those who died at the hands of someone with a hatred for the faith.

Among the conditions examined, then, are the motivations and mental states of both the victim and the persecutor, and these are not always easy to determine. If Fr. Pedro de Corpa, for example, was asleep when he was tomahawked, can it be truly said that he died voluntarily? Can we conclude that, because he clearly knew he was risking martyrdom when he first set out on the mission field, he thus died willingly? If a priest is executed by a right-wing dictator on charges of Socialist revolutionary activity, has he given his life for Jesus Christ, or for Karl Marx, or simply for justice? If a missionary bishop, while engaged in evangelism, is killed by bandits interested only in his worldly goods, is his death truly a martyrdom, or only a heinous crime?

I'm grateful that the resolution of such knotty issues is the task of the Church and not mine. In no way, then, do I intend for this work to prejudge the Church in matters of determining saints, sanctity, martyrdom, miracles, and related issues. I have no authority to do so. Instead, I simply wish to tell the stories of certain brave Catholic souls who died to bear witness to some aspect of Christ's truth. I gladly submit to the Church's judgments with regard to their status as martyrs in the formal sense.[4]

As I write this, it is the anniversary of Fr. Corpa's death for the faith. But it's also the vigil of the Triumph of the Cross.

I can think, then, of no more fitting day to offer this collection of martyrs' stories, for by their heroic witness, they remind us courageously of our Lord's promise: *Be faithful unto death, and I will give you the crown of life* (Rv 2:10).

Paul Thigpen
September 13, 2000

ONE

"AN IMAGE OF HIS MASTER"
Christ, the Model of Martyrdom

But if when you do right and suffer for it you take it patiently, you have God's approval. For to this you have been called, because Christ also suffered for you, leaving you an example, that you should follow in his steps.

1 PETER 2:20-21

By martyrdom a disciple is transformed into an image of his Master, who freely accepted death on behalf of the world's salvation; he perfects that image, even to the shedding of blood.

The Second Vatican Council, *Lumen Gentium*, V, 42

This very moment countless Catholics and other Christians throughout the world are languishing in prison, enduring brutal torture or facing violence and even death—simply for the sake of their faith.

Do you find that statement hard to believe? Consider this array of disturbing events and situations reported over the course of just a few recent weeks:

• A Catholic missionary brother, George Kuzhikandam, was beaten to death in India. The murder was the latest example of violence by Hindus against Christians in recent months, including nearly identical attacks on a number of priests, nuns, and laypersons. Christian leaders there also report frequent incidents of rape, looting, bombing, arson, exhumation of graves, and desecration of Christian churches.

- In Nigeria a Catholic priest, Father Clement Ozi Bello, was dragged from his car by a mob of angry Muslims. The assailants tied him up, gouged out his eyes, and killed him. Father Ozi Bello was from a Muslim family and had converted to the Christian faith. A bounty had been placed on the heads of all Catholic priests in his diocese.

- Father Rhoel Gallardo, a Claretian missionary in Malaysia, was tortured for days and then murdered by Muslim terrorists. Before killing him, they beat him repeatedly and tore out the nails of his index fingers and toes.

- In Yemen, Somali refugee and Christian convert Mohammed Omer was given a seven-day ultimatum by the government either to return to Islam or be executed for "apostasy." In Yemen, as in Saudi Arabia, all public expressions of Christian faith are illegal, as are evangelism and the possession of Bibles or other Christian literature.

- Father Jian Shurang, a Chinese Catholic priest, was sentenced to six years in prison for printing Bibles and other religious literature. In separate incidents: Auxiliary Bishop Jiang Ming Yuan of Hebei province was arrested and has not been heard from again. Twenty-four Chinese Catholics in another province were arrested, including a priest, twenty nuns, a seminarian, and two laypersons. The priest was severely beaten and suffered internal bleeding. The Catholic Church is outlawed in China; the Chinese government has tried to replace it with a national "church" without ties to Rome and controlled by the Communist regime.

- In the Moluccan Islands, Muslim forces continue the murder of Christians and widespread destruction of churches and Catholic institutions. Some local Muslim leaders have called for the extermination of "the Christian infidels," and thousands of armed men have come to the area intending to "cleanse the Moluccas of all Christians."

- In the Democratic Republic of the Congo, Catholic seminarian Gustave Amzati was killed in an attack on a major seminary. Rwandan and Ugandan forces supporting rebel factions in the country battle each other but are united in their systematic attacks on Catholic institutions and clergy.

- In Sudan, Muslim converts to the Christian faith are subject to the death penalty. After seventeen years of civil war, the Muslim government continues its long history of human rights violations against the Christians in the southern part of the nation. Catholic churches, schools, and clinics are frequently bombed. Governments have barred the delivery of humanitarian aid for the millions who have fled to refugee camps. Entire Christian villages have been overrun by soldiers, who then kill adults and adolescent boys and abduct children as slaves. Catholic bishops have reported the crucifixion of some Christian captives; most abducted children are forced to become Muslims.

This is just a gruesome sampling. The stories of horror go on and on, many of them carefully documented by international human rights organizations.[1] We'll never know how many martyrs have actually perished; countless among them have simply disappeared—the *desaparecidos,* as they have come to be called in Latin America.

What we know with certainty, however, is that the Christian martyrs of the past century, perhaps the majority of them Catholics, number in the millions, far more than those of any earlier century, more even than those of all the earlier centuries combined. One informed estimate puts the total at nearly twenty-seven million. And even though the mass killings of the first half of the century probably account for most of these deaths, this latest, darkest season of martyrdom is by no means over: The current annual count of Christian martyrs' deaths may well be more than 290,000.

Why the Silence About Martyrs?

The typical American Catholic would probably be stunned to hear of these outrages. And no wonder—most of the major news organizations have ignored the plight of these men, women, and yes, even children. Though victimhood seems to be a popular topic of discussion in our culture these days, only a handful of international religious news sources regularly report on contemporary victims of anti-Christian hatred.

Media Bias
In fact, the anti-Christian bias of much of the Western media not only minimizes or ignores the oppression of Christians; it actively contributes to a climate of fear and suspicion toward believers. As a case in point, consider the recent election of Mexico's new president, Vicente Fox, candidate of the Party of National Action. His victory ended the seventy-one-year rule of the Institutional Revolutionary Party (PRI), a group founded in

1929 by the vicious despot Plutarco Elias Calles, a man whose brutal treatment of Mexican Catholics earned him the nickname "the Mexican Nero."

While in control of the country, the PRI frequently resorted to terrorism to maintain its power. Denial of important religious freedoms remained a constant through its rule. Not surprisingly, in recent years the Catholic Church has recognized dozens of martyrs put to death by this regime.

When Fox's election finally brought to an end the PRI's long-oppressive power monopoly, we should have expected the Western press, self-proclaimed watchdog for human rights, to celebrate—or at least to report the events fairly. Instead, almost nothing was noted about the reasons why Mexicans might have wanted to throw off the PRI's rule. At the same time, when photos were snapped of Fox receiving Communion, as any normal Catholic would, news commentaries began to appear warning darkly of a "new intolerance."

A "new intolerance"? What about the "old intolerance"? What about the "current intolerance"—the outright brutality—that Catholics and other Christians suffer daily around the globe?

Perhaps we shouldn't be surprised; after all, this isn't a new problem. During the 1920s and 1930s, when the PRI's atrocities were at their worst, American journalists rarely reported on the events taking place there. Some were even bribed by Mexican officials to remain silent. As a result, most of the world knew little of the tragedy that was unfolding in that anguished nation. Perhaps the media silence and bias at that time explain in part why the United States actually backed the "Mexican Nero" and his brutal successor with arms, money, and moral support—but banned private arms shipments to those who revolted against such tyranny.[2]

Silence in the Church

Today's media silence about Christian martyrs is disturbing enough. Worse yet, however, is the silence in the churches. Even though these heroic believers deserve our gratitude and could serve us as inspiring examples of genuine faith, you've probably never heard a homily in Mass about them.

Reasons for the silence vary. The clergy tend to rely on the same inadequate news sources as their congregations. They may fear being perceived as "bigoted" toward people of other religions (or of no religion) if they talk about how some Muslims, Hindus, and atheists are killing Christians today. Or they may simply want to avoid a topic that seems to them unpleasant and uncomfortable.

If we consider the current subject matter of many homilies and religious publications, other reasons for the silence may grow clear as well. Too often, both clergy and laypeople have reduced the Christian faith to a smattering of happy-face platitudes—the tepid exhortation, in one form or another, to "be nice." For these people, the essence of the gospel seems to be that we should go along to get along, live and let live, never offend anyone, and show "tolerance" to the point of avoiding moral evaluations of any kind. References to heresy, sin, and especially hell are taboo.

Behind this parody of the Christian message—a caricature of the gospel that is inevitably fatal to authentic Catholic faith and practice—lies the assumption that all religions are basically alike, and of equal worth. One belief is as "true" as another, one moral standard as "right" as another. If truth and righteousness are relative categories—mere private opinions, subjective human creations rather than objective, universal realities—then who are we to make demands of anyone's intellect or will? A pragmatic "niceness" is all we have left if we want to keep the peace.

Venerable Cardinal John Newman once wisely observed: "No one is a martyr for an opinion; it is faith that makes martyrs." Not surprisingly, then, whenever indulgent pseudo-Christianity replaces faith as the faulty foundation of thinking, preaching, and writing, compromise replaces martyrdom, and genuine martyrs receive scant attention.

The martyrs simply don't fit into the "nice" box. They bleed all over it. People with their eyes gouged out and their fingernails torn off aren't "nice." In fact, their heroic sufferings and witness rip the mask of pretense right off the Gospel of Nice.

The Scandal of the Martyrs

The martyrs were people who lived their faith unashamedly, whatever the cost. They worshipped, they served, and they told others about Jesus Christ. They made moral judgments by his universal standards, and they acted and taught accordingly. They knew truth could not be relativized, and they refused to hide or deny it. They could not in good conscience go along to get along when they knew the path others were taking led to misery and damnation.

Is it any wonder that they offended people? In doing so, they only illustrated the scriptural warning that Christ and his gospel are a scandal, a stumbling block, an offense to those who reject him (see 1 Cor 1:23; 1 Pt 2:8).

The martyrs rebuked ambitious government officials and self-assured cultural elites, the wealthy and the powerful, familiar neighbors and faceless mobs. They publicly denounced political leaders for adultery and homosexual behavior. They told non-Christians that their religious beliefs were wrong and their gods false or even demonic. They tried to stop people from engaging in forms of murder and other crimes that the government had legalized.

How would preachers of the Gospel of Nice react to such bold actions in America today? We need not guess. Like the martyrs, Catholics and other Christians who dare to do these things in our contemporary culture are branded as zealots, fanatics, extremists, intolerant bigots, disturbers of the peace, and threats to the government and the people. Just keep your religion to yourself, their opponents insist; refrain from passing judgment, be quiet and support the system with your tax money. If you don't, any abuse you provoke will be merited, and we will silence you.

Is this an exaggeration? By no means. The press often reports acts of violence against abortion mills and their employees. But rarely do we hear about the Christian pro-life activists who have suffered for opposing the murders of the unborn.

Many have been arrested, imprisoned, and abused by police. Literally thousands of cases have been reported in the United States and Canada in which pro-lifers have become victims of violence ranging from destruction of property to murder. They have been physically assaulted with guns, automobiles, acid, hypodermic needles, and baseball bats. A number of activists and their families continue to receive anonymous threats that warn of death if they don't give up their advocacy for the unborn.[3]

The martyrs' enemies also sought to silence them. When these believers persisted in their refusal to be "nice," they were, in fact, silenced by death. But not forever. In dying, they joined the ancient succession of prophets who spoke for God and paid everything they had to deliver the message (see Lk 11:50-51; Heb 11:32-33). Now the voice of their blood, like the blood of their forerunner Abel, "is crying ... from the ground," and through their faith they are still speaking to us (see Gn 4:10; Heb 11:4).

Listening to the Martyrs

If the martyrs are speaking, how can we listen to them? Reading their stories is one way to listen. When we learn about the lives and deaths of these heroes, we soon find they have precious gifts to give us.

Perhaps the first significant insight we gain is that the martyrs were often quite ordinary men and women caught in extraordinary circumstances. In many ways they were everyday people like us, people who weren't looking for trouble and who prayed, even as Jesus had, that God might somehow spare them from it (see Lk 22:42). When the time of testing came, however, they opened themselves to divine gifts of grace that filled them with a more-than-human capacity to suffer and to conquer through their suffering.

"We have an idea of martyrdom which is too romantic and reduced to extraordinary stories that open the door to canonization," French Cardinal Roger Etchegaray recently observed. "But [martyrdom] should be the horizon in every Christian life."[4] Because the martyrs were so much like us, we can be confident that the faith that energized them, and the grace that sustained them, can energize and sustain us as well. Thus, their stories give us hope and deepen our trust in God.

"The death of the martyrs," said Pope St. Gregory the Great, "blossoms in the faith of the living." When we're tempted to compromise our faith, or give in to sin, or remain silent when the truth should be spoken, we need an infusion of the martyrs' strength and courage. That's why the writer of Hebrews recalls the sacrifices made by the martyrs and by the Lord they were imitating. He insists that they are a "great cloud of witnesses," surrounding us like cheering spectators as we run our own race of faith (see Heb 11:4–12:1). Don't give up, he exhorts; "in your struggle against sin you have not yet resisted to the point of shedding your blood," as they did (12:4). If we meditate on the victorious example set before us, we won't be likely to "grow weary or fainthearted" (12:3).

This spiritual dynamic explains the observation of Tertullian already cited that "the blood of Christians is seed." Though the martyrs' executioners sought to erase their influence on the world, instead they extended and intensified that influence. Jesus himself had said it would be so; he told his disciples that if they, like grains of wheat, would fall into the earth and die, they would multiply and bear much fruit (see Jn 12:24).

The Miracle of Martyrdom

Throughout Church history, miracles have occurred to draw attention to the faith, to demonstrate God's loving power, and to confirm the words of his messengers. Martyrs bear the same fruit because they are, in fact, a kind of miracle. Just as a physical miracle defies the laws of nature, a martyr defies the laws of human nature: To face death willingly is to overcome that most basic of human drives, the drive to self-preservation. "A martyrdom is a season of God's especial power in the eye of faith," insists Newman, "as great as if a miracle were visibly wrought."

Today, when the world hates the gospel as bitterly as ever, we desperately need the witness of the martyrs. All too often we worship comfort, and to one extent or another we've probably all been tainted by the Gospel of Nice. The martyrs come to us to make us uncomfortable, to judge us and call us to the greatest kind of love the world has ever witnessed: to lay down our lives for others by laying down our lives for the truth (see Jn 15:13).

Pope John Paul II has recognized this pressing need of our day. After quoting the words of Tertullian in his encyclical *Tertio*

Millennio Adveniente, he went on to summon the Church to recall, to record, and to recount the stories of the martyrs. "At the end of the second millennium," he wrote, *"the Church has once again become a Church of martyrs.* The persecution of believers—priests, religious and laity—has caused a great sowing of martyrdom in different parts of the world.... *This witness must not be forgotten."* [5] On May 7, 2000, as one way to fulfill our obligation to recognize the "new martyrs" of the past century, the Holy Father led the Jubilee celebration commemorating them.

Worthy of Honor

Yet the appropriateness of that celebration stems not only from the benefits we receive by remembering the martyrs. In addition, we should never forget that the martyrs are *worthy* of our veneration, our gratitude, our love. Would the believing family members of any one of them, while still living on earth, have ever ceased to honor them and be devoted to them after their sacrifice was completed? Impossible! Much less should we, the members of their spiritual family, ever forget them or fail to esteem them. Just as nations raise monuments to brave warriors fallen in battle, we should, as a matter of simple justice, grant the martyrs a place of honor in our churches and in our hearts.

Nor should we focus only on the martyrs of our day. For more than two thousand years now our elder brothers and sisters in the faith have offered their lives for God. We owe much to them; as Pope John Paul noted, the firm establishment of the Church and much of its development depended to a great degree upon "the *seeds sown by martyrs and the heritage of sanctity which marked the first Christian generations."* [6] Furthermore, even after the Church had been well-grounded and had extended throughout the world, it was the testimony of the martyrs that kept the Catholic faith alive and energetic in places where its enemies sought doggedly to eradicate it.

The fathers of Vatican II summed it up this way: "Since Jesus, the Son of God, manifested his love by laying down his life for us, no one has greater love than he who lays down his life for Christ and his brothers.... To give this supreme testimony of love to all men has been the calling of some Christians from the earliest times, and will always be. The Church, therefore, considers martyrdom as an exceptional gift and as the highest proof of love."[7]

From ancient times the Church has sought to recognize just how precious is this gift. Not only were the names of the martyrs carefully recorded and read publicly so that they would never be forgotten. In addition, their "birthdays"—that is, the dates of their holy deaths, when they were born into eternal life—were celebrated with great solemnity. Their remains were sought out and venerated, and Mass was celebrated at their tombs—the origin of the tradition that every altar should contain the relics of a saint. The places associated with their lives and deaths became places of pilgrimage. And their intercession was asked for by those who hoped to imitate their love and courage.

We turn now to look more closely at this "exceptional gift"— at some of the costly sacrifices that, as God's graces showered on the Church, have made possible her health, strength, and perseverance for two millennia. It's only fitting that we begin with the Divine Martyr, the crucified Son of God, who serves as both Source and Model for all the others.

The Man on the Cross

If you would understand the martyrs of the Catholic faith, begin by looking at that unmistakable symbol of the Catholic faith: the crucifix.

After two thousand years, the dark, stark image of the Crucified One still hangs upon the world and haunts it, abased and abandoned, bruised and bloodied, mocked and murdered. The crucifix is a sign of contradiction, for in it we see the scandal that is Jesus Christ.

To non-Christians, he is at worst a maniac or a fraud; at best he is, perhaps, a misunderstood reformer who should have known better than to challenge those in power. His tragic likeness is better left alone.

To non-Catholic Christians, he is the blessed Savior, and yet the sight of nails, thorns, and blood too often disturb. His cross is better left empty and clean, his portrait better painted as Victor.

To squeamish or revisionist Catholics, the tortured Victim is an embarrassment, a messy leftover from an outdated era. Better to replace him in churches with peaceful scenes of shepherd and sheep, to remove him altogether from the walls of hospitals, colleges, and schools. Why needlessly offend?

Yet even among those who see in him no scandal, passing by with hardly a thought of his pain, he may suffer a similar fate: ignored at church, forgotten at home, dropped from the necklaces that once kept him close to the heart. Not banished, but forsaken all the same.

And so once again—in hostility, discomfort, or apathy—the world despises and rejects the Man of Sorrows, and hides its face from the reminder of his passion (see Is 53:3). The crucifix—image of the Divine Martyr, God himself suffering and dying—becomes one of the *desaparecidos*, one of the ones who have disappeared.

His Nakedness, Our Own
Why does the world turn away from the Man on the cross? Why does it try to forget him? No doubt the ugliness of the scene can repel: The pain is palpable, the brutality grisly.

And yet the world often finds itself attracted to just such ugliness. Passing motorists slow down to gawk at a gruesome accident scene. Raucous crowds gather to cheer a barroom brawl. Violent video games, films, athletic events, and TV shows entertain children and adults alike who take pleasure in watching other people suffer. Our near-universal aversion to the Man on the cross cannot be accounted for simply by citing our fear of blood, because we also have a thirst for blood.

No—more than a visceral repulsion drives us away from the anguished Christ. If we take him seriously, at some level his agony begins to tear away comfortable but deceiving appearances so as to expose disturbing realities about the world and about ourselves. Just before his execution, Jesus told the Roman governor Pontius Pilate: "For this I was born, and for this I have come into the world, to bear witness to the truth" (Jn 18:37). Naked truth hangs suffering on the cross, and as it confronts us, we, too, are stripped, and Jesus' nakedness becomes our own.

What is that truth? we ask, echoing Pilate's own challenge. Jesus fell silent at the question, but the agony he went on to suffer bears eloquent witness to the profound reality he had come to make utterly clear: This world is fleeting and broken. It can find its ultimate meaning and final redemption only in the world to come.

Jesus' passion shouts that "all flesh is grass, and all its beauty is like the flower of the field. The grass withers, the flower fades" (Is 40:6-7). It testifies that our limited, transient life on earth cannot bear alone the glorious weight of what it means to be human; neither can we bear alone the tragic burden of our failure to be what we were created to be.

The pain of Jesus uncovers our pain. In him we can read the story of our own suffering and vulnerability—the crosses we must bear. And we resent that reminder of our weakness.

He Reveals Our Sin

But there is more. Jesus' innocence reveals, by contrast, our own culpability. Pilate examined Jesus before his crucifixion and concluded, "I find no guilt in him" (Jn 18:38, NAB). If we had been on trial that day, instead of Our Lord, what might have been the verdict?

We may not be murderers, but we have done our share of driving the nails of our selfishness into others' crosses. Family, friends, acquaintances, even total strangers have suffered at our hands, and if we are honest we must admit that even much of our own pain is self-inflicted. So we flee from the conviction of sin provoked by the dying Christ. "The world ... hates me," Jesus observed, "because I testify of it that its works are evil" (Jn 7:7).

Fleeing from judgment, we run into the sinister embrace of yet another reality demonstrated by the Crucifixion: In our wickedness, we are not alone. A darkness stalks the world, making use of humanity but not itself human, an invisible diabolical race so evil that it exceeds even our own insane capacity for malice. "Then Satan entered into Judas called Iscariot ... [to] betray him" (Lk 22:3-4). Is it any wonder that we shudder to see in the cross the macabre handiwork of our souls' great enemy?

Witness to Hope

At the same time, however, Jesus' suffering points beyond the nightmares of our world to a different world, one that makes those same demonic enemies tremble. An innocent Life lived in the truth, willingly offered up for the truth, forgiving those who have denied the truth, proclaims the reality of a good and holy God who transcends our broken world.

The truth is startling: The God who created the world and mourns its self-willed alienation from him has come to earth to die, to take on himself the burden we could not bear, so that we might return to him and be healed.

The Man on the cross declares that this God, to whom we owe everything, now demands for our own eternal good a loyalty higher than all other loyalties, a love deeper than all other loves. He is worth dying for, and if we must choose between life in this world without him or life in the next world with him, we must choose the latter at all costs.

In all these ways, then, the Crucified One is a sign of contradiction. In his passion and death, the world is judged and found wanting, the world is turned on its head. Its loves are exposed as vain infatuations; its wisdom is proved to be folly; its pride is cast down.

Yet the world cannot bear to be thus contradicted. So ever since it killed Jesus Christ for bringing it face to face with the truth, the world has loathed and secretly feared his tortured image—whether that image is carved in wood or in the suffering flesh of the martyrs.

Christ as Precedent and Pattern

To read the stories of Catholic martyrs is to gaze upon scenes that make Dante's *Inferno* seem tame by comparison. They were boiled in oil and laid on red-hot griddles, skinned alive and burned to ashes over slow fires. They were disemboweled, torn with hooks, and thrown to ravenous beasts.

When we read about such unimaginable horrors, we are tempted to ask why: Why was the world's antagonism toward them so cruel? Why did it demand of them so much blood, so much pain, so much humiliation? Why did the martyrs themselves deem it necessary to undergo such torments, when most of them could have been spared if they had only given in to their tormentors' demands?

Witness as Justice

If we could ask these questions of the killers and their victims, no doubt their answers would vary. "He challenged the authority of the state," the torturers might insist, or "She disturbed the peace." "I was only trying to serve God," the martyr might reply, or "I wanted to do good to others."

Yet behind all these answers would lie a single reality: The martyrs, seeking justice, told the truth, while their murderers, opposing justice, rejected the truth. The word *martyr*, after all, literally means "witness," and as the *Catechism of the Catholic Church* reminds us in speaking of martyrdom, "Witness is an act of justice that establishes the truth or makes it known."[8]

What was the truth that incited such hatred? The scandal of Jesus Christ.

"The martyr bears witness to Christ, who died and rose, to whom he is united by charity," the *Catechism* goes on to say. "He bears witness to the truth.... The acts of the Martyrs ... form the archives of truth written in letters of blood."[9]

Should we be surprised that the world hates and fears those who testify to Jesus' passion through their own life and death for his sake? Like a human crucifix, each one of them—men, women, even children—has become a disturbing image of the Truth the world desperately seeks to flee.

Jesus himself knew this would be the case. "If the world hates you," he warned his followers, "know that it has hated me before it hated you. If you were of the world, the world would love its own; but because you are not of the world, but I chose you out of the world, therefore the world hates you.... And you also are witnesses" (Jn 15:18-19, 27). In the passion of Jesus, then, we find the precedent for Christian martyrdom.

TWO

"CRYING IN THE WILDERNESS"
The Forerunner of Christ's Passion

In those days came John the Baptist, preaching in the wilderness of Judea, "Repent, for the kingdom of heaven is at hand." For this is he who was spoken of by the prophet Isaiah when he said, "The voice of one crying in the wilderness: Prepare the way of the Lord, make his paths straight."

MATTHEW 3:1-3

John the Baptist was beheaded and crowned with holy martyrdom. He was not bidden to deny Christ; and yet for confessing Christ he was slain; because the same Lord Jesus Christ had said, "I am the truth"; and because John was slain for the truth, he shed his blood for Christ.

Pope St. Gregory the Great, *Epistles*, 64

He was suffocating.

Nearly all his life he'd roamed the wild open spaces of the desert, bronzed by the sun, buffeted by the wind, alone and at liberty. But this cramped cell was dark, filthy, crawling with rats, infested with vermin, the foul air thick with the moans and curses and stench of the prisoners. To St. John the Baptist, a feral son of the wilderness, Herod's prison was a coffin.[1]

In the beginning, when John had first fled to the wastes for refuge, as his predecessor, Elijah, had done, the demons loosed on him had attacked in the open: by day, baring their fangs and claws and growling their taunts; by night, purring their temptations as they watched with cold eyes that never blinked. He fled, but they followed; he begged for mercy, but they howled in derision. At last he learned to fling in their faces his fasts and prayers and psalms, slashing them, burning them, and for a time they withdrew into the crevices and caves, licking their wounds and plotting.

In the silence left by their retreat, John could hear clearly at last. There among the rocks the Word of God overtook him.

Prepare the way of the Lord, make his paths straight! Every valley shall be filled, and every mountain and hill shall be brought low, and the crooked shall be made straight, and the rough ways shall be made smooth; and all flesh shall see the salvation of God.

The divine Word was a seed. John had to plant it carefully, in the richest soil of his soul, in the full sunlight of recollection. He had to water it countless days with his tears and dung it with his penance, the stinking refuse of sins forsaken and thus made fertile. In time the seed burst forth to blossom and bear its prickly fruit. He ate it and grew strong. He knew at last who he was, what he was to do, where he was to go, what he was to say.

At the Jordan
Then John whirled like a storm cloud out of the wilderness and thundered down on Judea.

Repent! The kingdom of heaven is at hand!

He had come of age, and the world had come of age, too. Heaven was done now with waiting. The kingdom of God was a wedding feast, and the world was to be courted. John was to wash her clean, get her ready to court, and in due time he would make the necessary introductions.

He had only to figure out who was the Bridegroom.

Raised on locusts and wild honey, forsaking bread and wine, wrapped in the borrowed skin of a camel, the brother of lizards and mountain goats knew little of niceties. God does not woo with sweet nothings. So John shouted at the Bride his invitation to bathe, and flung the bath water in her face.

You brood of vipers! Who warned you to flee from the wrath to come? Bear fruits that befit repentance....

The people flocked to the Jordan to hear him, but it was a mixed flock: Some settled in like turtledoves on the nest. Some circled like vultures around the victim. Some stood distant and motionless, like storks, watching and waiting. Priests and prostitutes, merchants and tax collectors, soldiers and fishermen. Tears mixed with taunts, repentance with revulsion, faith with fascination—only God himself could sort it all out.

For the most part, the priests and Levites were open, curious; the common people adoring and afraid. What did he demand of them? At first, no more than all the prophets had demanded: justice, mercy, humility before God. The warm and filled should share with the cold and hungry. The powerful should stop exploiting the weak.

The Pharisees and Sadducees, on the other hand, despised him. They were the privileged exceptions to his rules. They were clean, they insisted; cleanliness was their birthright. Abraham was their father.

God is able from these stones to raise up children to Abraham! Even now the axe is laid to the root of the trees; every tree therefore that does not bear good fruit is cut down and thrown into the fire.

How dare he speak of fire! The Sadducees denied that hell even existed. The Pharisees presumed that God had created it for everyone but them. After all, they kept the Law. Every tenth leaf of mint and dill they carefully plucked and proudly set aside for God. Yes, of course, in the meantime they devoured the poor and the poor in spirit. But they wiped their mouths and washed their hands when they were done.

Both Sadducee and Pharisee wanted to silence John. Yet they feared the mob, the clueless and accursed mob, who relished the sweet irony of their hypocrisy laid bare. So they waited and plotted. The mob was fickle, and would soon find another hero, and John would be dealt with.

Herod, the Romans' puppet who played king in Galilee, wasn't sure what to make of John. More than once he'd ordered his retinue to bear him to the edge of the crowds along the Jordan, near enough to hear but far enough to remain hidden. What he saw and heard first fascinated, then angered, then frightened him.

John was a holy man; that much Herod knew. And for a while, wickedness finds holiness intriguing, studying it with amused perplexity, too crippled to grasp its root, too feeble to taste its fruit. Unable to make sense of such exotic foliage, Herod had soon wearied of the game and began to look around for an axe. But he had to fell the prophet quietly. The mob worshipped this locust-eater; they might turn violent, and the Romans might blame him and find a new puppet.

Herod's wife, Herodias, his own brother's wife, wanted the prophet's head. It was all very well for him to give the crowds a bath—they stank and needed one—and she rather enjoyed hearing those pompous old prigs fume over his insults. But John had gone too far when he had pointed his bony finger through the curtains of the royal bedroom.

It is not lawful for you to have your brother's wife.

No one could call Herodias an adulteress and live. She screamed at her husband to wash her stained reputation in John's blood, but he was a coward. Why did he cringe before the crowds? She spat on them. They were dogs. She would spin her web and catch the gadfly that was stinging them all. She would have her revenge.

Meanwhile, the demons had returned to John, this time in the tirades of the hypocrites and the cheers of the crowd. "We will destroy you," they hissed. "We will make you our lord!" they cried. At the end of each day, after the last of the baptisms, he had to throw himself into the water to be cleansed again, to drown out their voices.

But all that changed the day the Bridegroom showed up.

The Bridegroom

In recent weeks John had announced his coming. Whatever rage the prophet had provoked by his rebukes, it was swallowed up by the excitement he stirred when he assured them that the promised Christ, the Anointed One of God, was at hand.

I am the voice of one crying in the wilderness, Make straight the way of the Lord!

The crowds demanded daily that he make good his promise. The leaders, both religious and political, took it as a threat. Was he setting himself up to be acclaimed as the Deliverer? Would he turn the throngs into an army? Would he take away the leaders' power and drive them out?

They sent secret messengers to ask him bluntly: "Who are you?" If he called himself the Christ, the Anointed One, they had grounds to move against him: They could accuse him of blasphemy against religion and sedition against Rome. He dashed their hopes.

I am not the Christ.

Was he the prophet Elijah come back from heaven, as the Scriptures had foretold? Was he the great Prophet who Moses had said would come?

No. I baptize you with water for repentance, but he who is coming after me is mightier than I, whose sandals I am not worthy to carry; he will baptize you with the Holy Spirit and fire. His winnowing fork is in his hand, and he will clear his threshing floor and gather his wheat into the granary, but the chaff he will burn with unquenchable fire.

They went away grumbling. He has a demon, they agreed.

Every day he scanned the faces of the crowd, searching for some clue that the Anointed One had come. How would he know when he saw him? How would the Christ reveal himself? Would he come right away in glory before the whole world, or would he come first to John in secret? And if a man came in secret, claiming to be the One, how could such a claim be judged?

Imposters had come and gone, bad actors on a grand stage whose tragic roles had cost men their lives. John had to be certain. If he were wrong, he might wed the people to a devil; he might push them toward damnation. He needed to see the glory, hear the glory, even if it were a secret glory, invisible and inaudible to everyone else. Before he could bear witness to the Anointed One, God himself had to bear witness to the Anointed One.

And so he did. Once again the Word of God overtook the prophet, this time a still, small voice within.

He on whom you see the Spirit descend and remain, this is he who baptizes with the Holy Spirit.

John had never seen the Holy Spirit—could anyone see him?—but faith grew, a swelling confidence that God himself would open his eyes to see things that no other man had ever seen.

He was startled the day his kinsman Jesus came to be baptized. John had known him since childhood; their mothers had been close friends as well as kinfolk. And of all the men he knew, this one alone had no need to wash his soul. He was a righteous man, a perfect man, so perfectly righteous that in his presence John always felt unworthy.

The prophet tried to turn him away. "I need to be baptized by you, and yet you come to me?"

Jesus, however, was firm.

Let it be so now; for thus it is fitting for us to fulfill all righteousness.

Jesus' Baptism

So John obeyed, half expecting the river to part in protest. Instead, the water embraced Jesus, clinging to him like an old friend, and as it ran down his face, it seemed all the more pure for having made the journey. The water itself had been cleansed, and John had been cleansed with it.

Suddenly the prophet's eyes and ears were aflame. A blazing white dove descended, burning a bright hole in the heavens as it flew, and it came to rest on Jesus' right shoulder. Then the earth itself seemed to melt in the heat of a fiery voice from the skies—not the thunder that follows the lightning, but rather the lightning itself made audible.

This is my beloved Son, with whom I am well pleased!

The baptism of Spirit and fire had begun.

Only God and the crowd know how long John stood there, possessed by the vision and the voice. When he was himself again—would he ever be himself again?—Jesus had slipped away through the noisy throng, in their eyes just one more penitent. Had no one else seen and heard what John had seen and heard? Still the voice within remained to sear his mind, kindling fires in unexpected places, each flame a torch to illuminate some dark cavern of his soul.

The Lamb of God

When Jesus came to the Jordan again, forty days later, the prophet knew his time had come. Raising his arms, he silenced the crowd. Then he pointed toward Jesus and shouted the words he'd been created to shout.

Behold the Lamb of God, who takes away the sin of the world! This is he of whom I said, After me comes a man who ranks before me, for he was before me. I myself did not know him; but for this I came baptizing with water, that he might be revealed to Israel.

They stood stunned and speechless as he told them of the vision and the voice. This ordinary-looking man? Some from Galilee recognized him: a carpenter and the son of a carpenter. Could anything good come out of Nazareth?

And I have seen and have borne witness that this is the Son of God.

Where were the attending angels, the hosts armed for battle, the trumpets calling the nation to war? This was John's Christ, John's Anointed One, John's Deliverer? Had the desert sun finally rotted the prophet's mind?

Confused and angry, the crowd began to disperse. Jesus himself went his way without comment. Soon John was left alone with his thoughts and with the few disciples who remained despite their perplexity.

The next day John was sitting silently by the river with two of his disciples when Jesus came walking by. John knew what he had to do. Looking Andrew in the eye, he pointed once more to Jesus and repeated the words of the day before.

Behold, the Lamb of God!

Reluctantly, Andrew understood. His eyes filled, a baptism of grief, and he stood, pulling his fellows up with him. They embraced John one last time, turned, and followed Jesus.

In the days following, John's disciples began trickling to

Galilee. He continued to baptize, but when Jesus appeared in Judea, the crowds went his way. John's friends complained; he silenced them with a long stare.

You yourselves bear me witness that I said I am not the Christ, but I have been sent before him. He who has the bride is the Bridegroom; the friend of the Bridegroom, who stands and hears him, rejoices greatly at the Bridegroom's voice; therefore this joy of mine is now full. He must increase, but I must decrease.

In Prison

Not long after, Herod's men showed up to bind him and take him away. Herodias' incessant taunts had finally pressed her husband to make his first move.

Now the daytime darkness of the prison cell was deepening into the blinding blackness of another night. The thought of his followers filled him with grief and dread. Where did they go? Why hadn't he heard from them? Were they safe from Herod? Had doubt and fear consumed them?

For a while the vermin on the walls were the only visitors. But not for long. Now there were vermin in his brain. The demons had returned, crawling inside his head, boring holes in his faith. "Did God really say...?"

Who was he to hear from heaven? Did he really think the King of the Universe would choose him from among all men to announce his kingdom? Were the visions from heaven or the ravings of a maniac? Desperately, he flung out a scroll of memories long furled, searching for words, pictures, anything he could recite to his tormentors to justify his life.

Memories

The angelic visitor ... yes, the angel. His life had begun with an angel. His father, a blameless old priest, saw the heavenly messenger at the altar, was struck dumb by the apparition. John's birth was prophesied; his aged, barren, righteous mother was promised a son, and God kept his promise.

The angel had said he would be filled with the Holy Spirit even from the womb. The angel had said he would be great before the Lord, he would go in the spirit and power of Elijah, he would make ready for the Lord a people prepared. The angel had even named him; the name meant "Gift of God." So began the scandal of his life; the kinfolk were already complaining about his name, wondering how the barren could be made to bear, asking what this child would be.

His father's prophecy at his birth had echoed that of the angel: John would be the prophet of the Most High, the preparer of his ways, the herald of the Dayspring from heaven. Even if he could doubt the angel, could he doubt his godly old father?

Suddenly his frantic thoughts were pierced by the raspy whisper of his name. Through a crevice in the cell wall he could hear the voice faintly, calling from outside. His men! They had stolen past the drunken guards in the moonless blackness.

What About Jesus?
First the queries about their whereabouts, what dangers they faced, what rumors were flying. Then the question that tore at his soul: What about Jesus?

When he'd heard of John's arrest, Jesus had withdrawn into Galilee. The crowds followed him there, and they were multiplying by the hour. The poor and the outcasts especially thrilled to his preaching, but the wealthy and proud as well had begged him to dine in their homes. Lately there were reports of miraculous cures, demons cast out, food mysteriously multiplied, even corpses brought back to life. Greeks and Romans scuffled with Jews for a chance to come close enough to touch him.

The Sadducees and Pharisees hated him. A good sign, thought John.

Yet the doubts chewed away at his confidence. Was the Anointed One coming to cleanse lepers, or to judge the world? Was he coming to bless the peacemakers, or to vanquish the wicked?

Wouldn't the true Christ have torn down the walls of this prison by now?

His disciples posed the same questions before he had the chance to ask them aloud. Were Andrew and the others led astray? Had they all been deceived? What if Jesus were deluded, or worse, a fraud?

They pressed the issue, and at last John faltered. Perhaps he was mistaken. Had Jesus himself ever claimed publicly to be the Christ? If his kinsman would not admit the claim, then all was lost.

So he sent two of his disciples to Jesus to ask him pointedly: "Are you he who is to come, or shall we look for another?"

The wait until they returned seemed like a lifetime, though only a day passed; all the years of hope and struggle paraded through his mind. Again his men crept through the darkness and whispered through the cracked wall.

Even as they had stood watching, they reported, Jesus had worked miracles: healings, exorcisms, other wonders. Still they had asked him John's question, and he had replied—gently, without reproach.

Go and tell John what you have seen and heard: the blind receive their sight, the lame walk, lepers are cleansed, the deaf hear, the dead are raised up, the poor have good news preached to them. And blessed is he who takes no offense at me.

It was an answer of sorts, but not as plain as John had hoped for. He thanked his disciples, dismissed them, and prayed for light.

Doubts

The ancient scroll of Isaiah fell open in his memory, the scroll that had prophesied his own ministry: *a voice crying in the wilderness.* Other words from the text began to press forward in his mind.

And the Spirit of the Lord will shall rest upon him, the spirit of wisdom and understanding, the spirit of counsel and might, the spirit of knowledge and the fear of the Lord ...

Then the eyes of the blind shall be opened, and the ears of the deaf unstopped; then shall the lame man leap like a hart, and the tongue of the dumb sing for joy ...

The Spirit of the Lord God is upon me, because the Lord has anointed me to bring good tidings to the poor ...

The age-old words began to rekindle his faith. Isaiah's book was finding its fulfillment. Hadn't the Christ come to heal as well as to judge?

Yet the demons were not so easily silenced. Wasn't it a little suspicious that the man John claimed was the Christ should be his kinsman? Could he truly believe his childhood playmate was the Son of God?

His childhood playmate ... odd memories came rushing back, faint recollections of stories he had overheard his mother and father telling relatives when he had been too young to understand or even to ask questions. Reports of prodigies surrounding his kinsman's birth, more remarkable than the events surrounding his own.

The same angel who had visited John's father, so they said, had come to Jesus' mother, again to her husband, had announced his coming, had even named the child, as he had named John. The name meant "God is salvation." Just as John's father had prophesied, so also had Jesus' mother, words about exalting the lowly and filling the hungry with good things.

Jesus' mother. She was so much like her son—no other woman so pure had ever lived. John thought of them both, blessed mother and son, and felt a stirring within. It grew stronger, till he trembled all over, till his heart began to pound, till at last he found himself leaping in the darkness, a sudden explosion of joy lifting him from the floor of the prison cell.

My soul magnifies the Lord, and my spirit rejoices in God my Savior!

So also had he once leapt for joy in his mother's womb, even then testifying to the Christ, though of course he had no recollection of it. The same Spirit who had filled him then was filling him once again.

Martyrdom

When the guards came for him soon after, he was ready. On the way to the place of execution, they spilled out the whole obscene story.

Herod had thrown himself a birthday party, with Herodias' daughter providing entertainment for his guests with a lewd dance. Herod's lust had been so inflamed by his own niece that he'd made a rash oath, in the presence of the revelers, that he'd grant her anything she asked.

Herodias had wasted no time. She'd prompted her daughter to call for John's head, served on a silver platter, as the last course of the birthday feast. Herod had whined; Herod had pouted; Herod had professed to be sorry—not with remorse for his wickedness, but with regret that he'd been tricked into risking a riot.

Yet his vanity demanded that he keep up the appearance of integrity before his guests. After all, he had sworn an oath. So he gave the command, and it was done. John's disciples came and took the body, to bury it in the wilderness he loved.

John was a burning and shining lamp, and you were willing to rejoice for a while in his light.

When the Bridegroom heard that his friend was dead, he got in his boat, left the crowds, and went to be alone.

THREE

"THE CUP THAT I DRINK, YOU WILL DRINK"
Martyrs of the First Generation

And Jesus said to them, "The cup that I drink you will drink; and with the baptism with which I am baptized, you will be baptized."

MARK 10:39

Let us honor the apostles as the Lord's brothers, who saw him face to face and ministered to his passion.... Let us also honor the martyrs of the Lord chosen out of every class, as soldiers of Christ who have drunk his cup and were then baptized with the baptism of his life-bringing death, to be partakers of his passion and glory: of whom the leader is Stephen, the first deacon of Christ and apostle and first martyr.

St. John of Damascus,
Exposition of the Orthodox Faith, 4, 15

They had seen it with their own eyes, heard it with their own ears: a brilliant light, a roar from the skies, an enveloping cloud, a close encounter with two visitors from another world. But who would believe them? After all, fishermen are known for their tales.

More incredible still was the identity of the extraterrestrials, or perhaps we should call them post-terrestrials—beings whose origin was earthly, but whose current residence was not. They were by no means alien. Every Jew knew them, and knew them well, if only by reputation: Moses, the venerated giver of the divine Law, and Elijah, the greatest of God's ancient prophets (see Mt 17:1-21; Lk 9:28-43).

They had come to see Jesus. And when they had, God himself had borne witness to him, thundering out of the cloud: *This is my Son, my Chosen; listen to him!* To confirm the testimony, Jesus himself had been transfigured, his face and clothes so dazzling white that at first the fishermen thought the sun had risen at midnight on the mountaintop.

If ever there was a time when the apostles Peter, James, and John thought the kingdom had come, it was then. As usual, impetuous Peter spoke out for them all when he expressed his pleasure that the day of glory had arrived, and offered to build shelters so Jesus, Moses, and Elijah could settle down on the mountain. But God had other ideas.

The Old Testament saints disappeared as quickly as they had appeared. The day of glory was delayed. Jesus led the three disciples back down into the valley—where the demoniac, and a faithless and perverse generation, awaited them.

Why had the visitors come? What thrilling message from heaven had they brought? What great events had they planned with Jesus? Was the kingdom at last about to appear? When the four men had nearly reached the place where they'd left the others, Peter found the courage, or perhaps the brashness, to ask.

Jesus' reply was both sober and sobering. They had talked, he said simply, of his death, which would soon take place in Jerusalem.

Perplexed Apostles

What cruel joke was this? they wondered. Jesus had no need to die. Yes, his enemies were plotting. But if the great crowds that sought him out could see and hear what the fishermen had just seen and heard, wouldn't they all believe? The Pharisees and Sadducees had asked for a sign from heaven (see Mt 16:1); if they too could have witnessed it, wouldn't even they have believed? Peter could have built three thrones on the spot, and together they could have ruled God's kingdom right there on the mountain.

The Lord God had claimed Jesus as Son. The two most revered figures of Jewish sacred history, the captains of the Law and of the Prophets, had sought out his fellowship. Why, then, had it happened atop a desolate mountain, in the middle of the night, far from the eyes of the nation? Why did God hide his glory?

Then Jesus' own words came back to them. They already have Moses and the prophets, he had said. Let them listen to what God has already spoken through them. If they truly believe the witness of Moses, they will believe Jesus, for Moses wrote about him. But if they reject what God has already told them through Moses and the prophets, even someone who has come back from the dead could not convince them (see Lk 16:29-31; Jn 5:46).

Death—why did he keep talking of death? Tell no one what happened, he insisted as they came down the mountain, until the Son of Man is raised from the dead (see Mt 17:9). Why had God summoned Moses and Elijah to come all the way from the underworld to speak of death? Only a few days before, Jesus had insisted that he had to go to Jerusalem to suffer and die at the hands of the religious leaders there. On the third day he would rise again. But Peter had rebelled at the very idea—had even dared to rebuke the Master.

"God forbid, Lord!" he'd shouted. "This shall never happen to you!" Then had come Jesus' own stunning rebuke in reply—words Peter would never forget.

Get behind me, Satan! You are a hindrance to me; for you are not on the side of God, but of men (Mt 16:23).

The reproach silenced and crushed him, and his mind reeled so that he hardly heard the rest of what the Lord had said.

If any man would come after me, let him deny himself and take up his cross and follow me. For whoever would save his life will lose it, and whoever loses his life for my sake will find it. For what will it profit a man, if he gains the whole world and forfeits his life?... For the Son of man is to come with his angels in the glory of his Father, and then he will repay every man for what he has done (vv. 24-27).

In those brief words lay the key to their destiny, and the promise that would make worthwhile all the horrors they would have to suffer so that such a destiny could be fulfilled. Both death and glory—in that order. For the moment, however, such thoughts seared Peter's mind. He couldn't bear them, so he tossed them aside.

Mysterious Warnings

In the days following, not only Peter but all the twelve struggled as Jesus continued his grim predictions.

Let these words sink into your ears; for the Son of man is to be delivered into the hands of men (Lk 9:44).

Behold, we are going up to Jerusalem, and everything that is written of the Son of man by the prophets will be accomplished. For he will be delivered to the Gentiles, and will be mocked and shamefully

*treated and spit upon; they will scourge him and kill him, and on
the third day he will rise* (Lk 18:31-33).

*The hour has come for the Son of man to be glorified. Truly, truly,
I say to you, unless a grain of wheat falls into the earth and dies, it
remains alone; but if it dies, it bears much fruit* (Jn 12:23-24).

So many warnings, yet they simply couldn't understand; the
meaning was hidden from them. They were afraid to ask him to
explain it further (see Lk 9:45; 18:34). So they blocked out
thoughts of death with thoughts of glory alone, arguing over
who would take the places of honor in the coming kingdom,
begging to pronounce judgment on their enemies even now
with fire from heaven, rejoicing over the retreat of the demons
(see Lk 9:46, 54; 10:17).

Occasionally one of them seemed to catch a glimpse of what was
in store. When Lazarus' death prompted Jesus to return to Judea,
where his enemies threatened to stone him, most of the disciples
protested that it was too dangerous. Yet Thomas declared to the
others, "Let us also go, that we may die with him" (Jn 11:16).

Such moments were rare. Even on the night the Lord was
betrayed, when his passion was at hand and he had so much to
say before he was taken from them, they wasted time arguing
again over who would be the greatest in the kingdom. He
promised them that they would indeed have their thrones one
day, but tried one last time to prepare them for the horrors that
were now only hours away (see Lk 22:24-30).

*You will all fall away because of me this night; for it is written,
"I will strike the shepherd, and the sheep of the flock will be scattered"* (Mt 26:31).

Once again failing to understand, Peter spoke up. "Though
they all fall away because of you, I will never fall away.... Even if
I must die with you, I will not deny you" (Mt.26: 33, 35). And
the rest insisted that he spoke for them all.

Before the night was over, of the twelve would-be martyrs, one had betrayed him, one had denied him, and all had fled, leaving him alone to suffer and to die. The Scriptures were fulfilled.

Too Soon for Martyrdom

It was, in fact, too soon for their martyrdom. If they were to bear a full testimony to Christ with their blood, they had to witness more than his sinlessness, his wisdom, his miracles, even his divinity. They had to behold the terror of his death and the glory of his resurrection.

And so they did. Not many days later, the disciples stood at a fearful distance to witness the stark reversal: Once clothed with brilliance in the nighttime upon the mountain, now the Master was clothed in darkness in the daytime upon the cross. The sun hid its face from the crime, a new and gruesome transfiguration that turned the Lord's familiar countenance into an unrecognizable mass of bloody anguish.

So much of what he'd predicted had now come to pass. How utterly horrifying, then, was his prophecy of the disciples' own future.

The cup that I drink you will drink; and with the baptism with which I am baptized, you will be baptized (Mk 10:39).

They went into hiding. How long before Jesus' enemies would come for them as well? Now that he was gone, would they be willing to die for a memory only—for the message of a kingdom that had never come?

Resurrection

Their terror and grief overshadowed the words they had never understood in the first place.

They will scourge him and kill him, and on the third day he will rise (Lk 18:33).

Tell no one the vision, until the Son of man is raised from the dead (Mt 17:9).

So Jesus himself had to return, both to remind and to explain, both to show and to tell, the meaning of his resurrection. The empty tomb was not enough; the word of the angels was not enough; the stunning testimony of the women was not enough. They had to see him face to face: twice in the Upper Room at Jerusalem, once on the road to Emmaus, again by the seaside in Galilee, at last on the Mount of Olives (see Lk 24:10-49; Jn 20:19-21:14; Acts 1:1-12).

O foolish men, and slow of heart to believe all that the prophets have spoken! Was it not necessary that the Christ should suffer these things and enter into his glory? (Lk 24:25-26).

Beginning with Moses and the prophets, with whom he had counseled in glory that day on the mountaintop, he interpreted for them all the Scriptures that had prophesied his life, death, and resurrection (see Lk 24:27, 45).

Thus it is written, that the Christ should suffer and on the third day rise from the dead, and that repentance and forgiveness of sins should be preached in his name to all nations, beginning from Jerusalem. You are witnesses of these things. And behold, I send the promise of my Father upon you; but stay in the city, until you are clothed with power from on high (Lk 24:46-49).

First death, then glory. That was to be their message and their destiny. Christ had died for the world and then entered into glory. All must die to self if they would enter into glory with him. The disciples would die as his witnesses and enter into his glory.

At last they understood. Standing once again on a mountaintop, Jesus was once again transformed, once again joined by two visitors from another world. But this time the visitors were angels, and they spoke not of his sorrowful death but of his glorious return. This time they remained while he departed. And this time the disciples went back down the mountain alone—but not for long (see Lk 24:50-52; Acts 1:1-11).

Power to Be Witnesses

On the appointed day he came as promised—the Holy Spirit, Power himself, the power they had lacked when they had fled on the night of his betrayal. Not only on the twelve did he come—the traitor having been replaced with God's own choice—but on 120 of them: Mary, the mother of the Lord, and the women, and others who had joined them as witnesses from the beginning. Just as the martyred Baptist had promised, their martyred Lord now baptized them in the Spirit and fire, casting a burning tongue upon each of them so that he could speak through them (see Lk 3:16). Now they were ready, now they were able, to be his witnesses, his martyrs—in Jerusalem, in Judea and Samaria, and all the way to the ends of the earth (see Acts 1:1–2:47).

A divine seed had been buried; the first fruits of his harvest now appeared. The one Teacher, Preacher, Healer, Exorcist, Miracle Worker had been succeeded by 120 who multiplied his works, and all Jerusalem was in an uproar.[1]

Jesus' enemies were dumbfounded. The rumors of his resurrection they had, of course, dismissed out of hand, just as they had the reports of his miracles. No doubt, they murmured, his friends had stolen the body, so that even in death the deceiver had continued to deceive. But what was to be made of these illiterate followers of his—fishermen, tax collectors, women— who had dropped their nets, moneybags, and spindles and taken to disturbing the peace?

It was bad enough that these scoundrels filled Jerusalem with his scandalous ideas. Much worse, however, they were pointing the finger of blame for his death, rousing the rabble against the Pharisees, Sadducees, priests, and scribes. The dangerous revolution the religious leaders had hoped to forestall by killing the Carpenter was well under way at the hands of his disciples.

There was only one thing to do: silence the leaders. Make an example of them, and that would silence the rest.

Attempts to Silence Them

Two of the chief agitators, Peter and John, were caught committing an incendiary act: the public healing of a man who had been lame since birth. They were promptly arrested, questioned, and commanded to stop speaking in the name of Jesus. The men refused: "We cannot but speak," they insisted, "of what we have seen and heard" (Acts 4:20). They were threatened, but no one dared punish them yet for fear of the crowds now coming under their spell. They were released.

Again the new preachers stirred the crowds; thousands believed their witness and were baptized in the name of the Carpenter. The high priest, in a jealous rage, fearful of losing his authority, threw them into prison. Miraculously, they slipped out by night, right through the locked doors and past the heavy guard. Caught preaching yet again, again they were arrested, brought before the religious council, and threatened.

"We must," they said simply, "obey God rather than men.... We are witnesses" (Acts 5:29, 32).

The high priest and council were enraged to find these Galilean peasants so incorrigible. Though the murder of Jesus hadn't solved the problem of Jesus, that lesson had been lost on them; they decided to kill his followers as well. Yet one Pharisee of a wiser sort suggested that they restrain themselves. If the annoying little movement was a work of God (at this the council hissed), the holy leaders of God's people would hardly want to be found fighting him. If, on the other hand, it were something else, it would soon go the way of other religious fads.

Reluctantly, the council agreed. But they had the apostles beaten, and threatened them once more for good measure.

The preaching intensified and the miracles multiplied; even some of the priests were now bewitched. A shudder swept through the religious establishment; their status and power were slipping away. Something had to be done right away. The opportunity came with the emergence of a new tier of leadership in the infant Church: the deacons.

St. Stephen

For centuries, a fissure had run down the middle of the Jewish community, separating Jews deeply influenced by Greek culture from those more traditionally grounded in ancient Hebrew ways. The gospel had not yet had sufficient time to heal that tear among the new Jewish Christians, and a dispute erupted over the daily distribution of food to the widows in the community. The Hellenists, as the Greek-speakers were called, complained that the Hebrews overlooked them.

The apostles lacked the time to involve themselves in such matters, so they called for seven men to deal with the problem, "men of good repute, full of the Spirit and of wisdom" (Acts 6:3). Among these new deacons—the term means "servants"—was Stephen, "full of faith and of the Holy Spirit" (v. 5). The seven were ordained by the apostles and set to work.

Stephen was a humble man, willing to wait tables for his elderly sisters in the Lord. He was well situated to be their advocate: a Hellenist himself, he bore a Greek name well known among local Jews with Greek names. Yet he was much more than a waiter. The Spirit worked through him with great grace and power, performing miracles that grabbed the attention of all Jerusalem, and preaching the gospel in a way that could not long be ignored by its opponents.

Hellenist Jews from Rome, Africa, and Asia Minor living in Jerusalem felt most keenly the heat of his spiritual flame, though many were blind to its light. They took to disputing him publicly. After all, the Hellenists prided themselves on their intellectual accomplishments, their cosmopolitan culture. They claimed the ethereal Greek philosophy of Plato as their own no less than the earthy diatribes of the Hebrew prophets. How dare one of their kinsmen embarrass them by succumbing to this illiterate, provincial sect, worshipping a dead criminal, ranting about a resurrection!

Yet, despite all their training in rhetoric, logic, and philosophy, they were bested by the eloquent waiter. Stephen silenced their platonic platitudes with his gripping eyewitness testimony of One among them who had lived purely, died nobly, and risen again in glory. In debate, a man who has walked and talked with Truth himself is never at the mercy of men with nothing more than educated opinions.

The First Christian Martyr

As had the apostles who appointed him servant of the Church, Stephen bore witness with his hands and his voice. He would be first to bear witness with his blood. His Hellenist opponents, humiliated by his wisdom, resorted to less intellectual strategies.

Worthless men were suborned to bear false witness against him. "We have heard him speak blasphemous words against Moses and God," they claimed. "This man never ceases to speak words against this holy place and the law; for we have heard him say that this Jesus of Nazareth will destroy this place, and will change the customs which Moses delivered to us" (Acts 6:11, 13-14).

Perhaps they were the same lying rogues who had appeared before the high priest at Jesus' own trial before the council, for the same accusations had been hurled at him (see Mt 26:59-61). There was just enough truth in what they said to complicate Stephen's defense. Difficult sayings were taken out of context and twisted; a key word or two was changed to alter meanings dramatically.

In such a sensational setting, inattentive hangers-on, used to seeking excitement more than truth, might well recall a few of these words from Stephen's preaching. Their imaginations could easily supply the rest. Confirming the charges, they would help provoke another spectacle to relieve their boredom.

As it turned out, they had no need to stir up excitement; Stephen's charismatic preaching was equal to the task. Given a chance to respond to the charges against him, he took the stand, shining with the glory of the risen Lord himself. His defense was brief, elegant, to the point. He offered them a summary of salvation history, showing how the story of his people found its climax in the person of Jesus. But the recurring theme of that story nonetheless was their rejection of God, his plan, and ultimately his Christ.

"You stiff-necked people, uncircumcised in heart and ears!" he shouted. "You always resist the Holy Spirit. Which of the prophets did your fathers not persecute?"

The Spirit who had rested on the Baptist and on Jesus was speaking, repeating himself yet one more time with a harsh mercy that might still provoke some to repentance. "They killed those who announced beforehand the coming of the Righteous One, whom you have now betrayed and murdered, you who received the Law as delivered by angels and did not keep it!" (see Acts 7:51-53).

The proud listeners simply could not bear the burden of their guilt. A murderous rage contorted their faces, grinding their jaws like millstones void of grist. Stephen's moment of death and glory had come.

"The Son of Man, Standing"

He looked to the heavens for help, and there he saw, as Isaiah had seen, the Lord arrayed in brilliant splendor. "Behold, I see the heavens opened," his voice rang out, "and the Son of man standing at the right hand of God" (Acts 7:56).

For centuries to come, the theologians would ponder the import of his words: In every other vision of God portrayed in the Scriptures, the Son is *seated* at the right hand of the Father. Such was the posture of One who ruled and judged. Why, then, was Jesus standing when Stephen saw him?

St. Ambrose of Milan summed up the wisdom of the Fathers on the matter. "Christ sits as Judge of the living and the dead; he stands as his people's Advocate," he reasoned. So when Stephen saw the Lord, "he stood then as a Priest, while he was offering to his Father the sacrifice of a good martyr; he stood, as the Umpire, to bestow, as it were, upon a good wrestler the prize of so mighty a contest."[2]

The vision completed, God's lamb was brought to the altar. The hypocrites and their mob rushed upon him, screaming and stopping their ears to seal themselves against the truth. No need to pronounce a verdict; with their own ears they had heard him blaspheme, just as they had heard Jesus. According to their grisly custom, they seized him violently and dragged him to a precipice outside the city to be bound, cast down, and stoned.

The false witnesses cast the first few stones, and the innocent blood began to flow. Just as on the cross the Son of God had committed himself to the Father, so the servant now committed himself to the Son. "Lord Jesus," he prayed, "receive my spirit" (Acts 7:59).

Forgiveness

The stones rained down. Stephen looked at his killers with a supernatural compassion and with his last words conformed himself most perfectly to the image of his Master. "Lord," he begged, "do not hold this sin against them."

Commenting on this moment, St. Gregory Nazianzus later wrote, "Among men of ancient and modern days, each is considered to have had some special success, having received from God some particular virtue.... Now the special distinguishing mark of Stephen ... was the absence of malice."

When the martyr had prayed for his murderers, St. Luke tells us gently, "he fell asleep" (Acts 7:60).

He was the first Christian to wrestle the devil and win the prize, the laurel wreath from Christ's own hand. Thus his name had prophesied his destiny, for Stephen means, in his native Greek tongue, "the one who is crowned."

Stephen's death stirred up a whirlwind of hatred against the young Church. As persecution drove the new believers out of town, it scattered the seed of his blood throughout Judea and Samaria, Phoenicia and Syria and Cyprus. Wherever they fled, they preached to their new neighbors, a swirling cloud of witnesses settling in new soil.

So began the mission to the Gentiles, the planting of a vast harvest that would transform the face of the Church. An energetic evangelist named Philip and his charismatic daughters took the Word to the Samaritans, the despised half-breeds whom James and John had once thought to consume with fire from heaven. An angel sent Philip next down the desert road to Gaza, where he met the treasurer of the queen of Ethiopia, returning from a pilgrimage. His mind was open and his spirit hungry; by the time he went home he belonged to Christ, and Africa was among the first to hear the gospel.

We can understand, then, why St. John Chrysostom would later celebrate the first Christian martyr's death with these words: "Let Stephen be killed, the church of Jerusalem dispersed in confusion: for out of it go forth burning brands that, in spreading themselves, spread their flame. For in the church of Jerusalem, as it were, burning brands were set on fire by the Holy Spirit when they had all one soul and one heart toward God. When Stephen was stoned, that pile of brands suffered persecution; they were dispersed, and the world was set on fire."[3]

St. James, the Brother of John

Despite the initial scattering of the faithful, the twelve remained at Jerusalem for a while. They remained in grave danger, but the persecution was inconsistent and unpredictable. Hostility toward them seemed to wax and wane according to the personal whims, political agendas, and professional preoccupations of the authorities.

Even so, a new wave of terror began when Herod seized James, the apostle in Jesus' inner circle who, with his brother John and Peter, had witnessed the Lord's transfiguration on the mountain. God had arranged a miraculous prison break for the other two, and would do so again for Peter in the days to come. Yet there would be no miracle of deliverance for James; his hour had come.

Scripture tells little about the last years and heroic deaths of the twelve. Most of what we know with any certainty comes down from other sources, generally reliable but not always in agreement. St. Luke tells us simply that Herod had James executed by the sword (see Acts 12:1-2).

The second-century bishop Clement of Alexandria offered a few more details. He told the story as he had received it from those who had lived before him, early Christians of the generation right after the apostles. According to Clement, James bore such eloquent testimony to Christ in his trial that the official who escorted him to the judgment seat was deeply moved as he listened. The man became a Christian on the spot, made his own public confession of faith, and was condemned along with James.

The two were led away to be beheaded. Feeling remorse for having taken part in the apostle's mistreatment, the condemned official begged James' forgiveness before he died. "Peace be with you," James replied, kissing him as a sign of his pardon, and of the Lord's pardon as well. Then they laid down their lives together.

Herod found that his crime pleased those who hated the Church, so he had Peter arrested as well. As it turned out, Peter's hour had not yet come, but Herod's had.

Soon after these latest misdeeds, the ruler appeared publicly at some pagan festival games in honor of Caesar, wearing a gleaming silver robe that caught the sunlight and dazzled his admirers. As he delivered an oration from the throne, his flatterers began to shout, "The voice of a god, and not of man!" True to his character, the vain, crowned fool basked in these blasphemies.

Enough was enough. Heaven's avenging angel struck him on the spot; he had seized for himself the glory that belongs to God alone. Pain pierced his heart and exploded throughout his abdomen. Belatedly, Herod cried out words of regret, but the deed was done. He was carried to the palace and died there after five days of horrible agony, his insides consumed by worms.

The Other Apostles

According to the oldest traditions, the other apostle named James, the kinsman of the Lord, was the next to offer his blood. Having been chosen bishop of Jerusalem, he was a natural target for the Church's enemies. Arrested and ordered to renounce publicly his faith in Christ, instead he preached the gospel boldly, making more converts from the crowd.

His adversaries were enraged by such impudence. They took him up on the pinnacle of Jerusalem's great temple and threw him down. Finding that he was not yet dead, they began to stone him. At last a fuller standing by took up the club he used to beat out clothes and struck the martyr a fatal blow to the head. So James the Just was released at last to meet his kinsman and Lord.

Afterward, the other apostles left Jerusalem to fulfill the mandate they had been given: the gospel was to be taken to "the end of the earth" (Acts 1:8). Legends abound about where they preached and met their deaths, though some traditions are more trustworthy than others.

Andrew, they say, preached in the regions north of the Black Sea, but he died at last in Greece, where the Roman governor crucified him on a cross in the shape of an X. Andrew was bound rather than nailed to the wood, to assure that his suffering would be prolonged. Yet, during the long hours of his agony he preached from the cross and exhorted those who executed him to embrace Christ.

Bartholomew, according to the Roman martyrology, preached in India and Armenia, where he was skinned alive and beheaded by King Astyages. Other ancient traditions find him taking the gospel to Egypt, Mesopotamia, and Persia as well before his martyrdom.

Simon and Jude, insists one ancient text, preached in Persia and were killed there for their faith.

According to the Roman martyrology, Matthew preached and died in Ethiopia. He was crucified there on a T-shaped cross, then beheaded with a battle-ax.

Another ancient text tells how Matthias, who took the place of Judas among the twelve (see Acts 1:15-26), preached in Judea and Cappadocia and on the shores of the Caspian Sea, where he suffered countless persecutions. Some said he was stoned and beheaded in Colchis, on the Black Sea.

Early traditions report that Philip preached in Greece and was crucified at Hierapolis in Asia Minor, also on a T-shaped cross.

Thomas, some say, took the gospel all the way to Parthia and then to India. To this day the Syrian Christians of the Malabar region of India, who call themselves "Christians of St. Thomas," insist that they were first evangelized by him. For his efforts he, too, was rewarded with martyrdom: At the city of Mylapore, near Madras, he built a new church with his own hands, but was shot with arrows and killed by the spear of a pagan priest.

John and Revelation
Alone among the twelve, St. John seems to have escaped a violent death for his faith. He did indeed imitate his Lord's suffering, but his was a slow martyrdom, stretched out over a lifetime.

One Western tradition reports that the Roman emperor Domitian, a vain despot who demanded to be worshipped as Lord and God, ordered John to be thrown into a cauldron of boiling oil outside the city of Rome. The apostle emerged from the oil unharmed, but his sufferings were far from over: Domitian then banished him to the island of Patmos.

Ancient tradition throughout the Church goes on to affirm that this apostle was thus the same John who wrote the Book of Revelation while in exile. There, on that desolate island in the Aegean Sea, the plight of the persecuted Church was never far from his mind. Jesus commanded him to encourage the suffering Christians of the seven churches of Asia and commended the martyrs among them (see Rv 1–3).

In John's vision, he beheld under the altar in heaven "the souls of those who had been slain for the word of God and for the witness they had borne" (Rv 6:9). He prophesied as well about the coming of the "Beast" who would "make war on the saints and ... conquer them" for a season (Rv 13:7). Yet his words were full of hope, declaring that he had seen Christ's final victory over the forces of evil that had rejected God and his truth. Ever since John's revelation was published, Christian martyrs have held fast to the promise of the Lord it contains: "He who conquers, I will grant him to sit with me on my throne, as I myself conquered and sat down with my Father on his throne" (Rv 3:21).

The traditions about the apostles recorded outside of Scripture, even those in substantial agreement, cannot be proven accurate beyond all doubt, given our present level of historical knowledge. Yet, allowing for considerable embroidering of the facts, two claims seem consistent throughout the stories: The apostles obeyed Christ's command to live the rest of their lives as his witnesses; and they paid dearly, though willingly, for their testimony. By his grace, they were able to drink the bitter cup their Lord had drunk.

Meanwhile, in the case of Saints Peter and Paul we can be more confident of the record. No doubt because the early Church recognized the two men as holding extraordinary positions of leadership in the Christian community, their deaths were carefully noted and vividly recalled. That both apostles suffered martyrdom in Rome at the hand of the Roman emperor Nero is thus affirmed by a tradition that from early times remained universal and unchallenged by any contrary claims.

St. Paul
The Witness "Untimely Born"

The great irony of Paul's ministry and martyrdom, of course, is his role in the martyrdom of Stephen. We first meet him in the book of Acts—his name then is Saul—not as an apostle or even a disciple of Jesus, but rather as his enemy. Saul assumes a ghastly responsibility for the lying murderers of Stephen: He agrees to watch over their clothes so they can unencumber themselves for casting their stones (see Acts 7:58-8:1).

Saul was no innocent bystander. St. Luke tells us explicitly that the young man gave his consent to the crime (see Acts 8:1). Worse yet, in the unrest sparked by Stephen's death, Saul became an aggressive persecutor himself, invading Christian homes, dragging off both men and women to prison, prowling from city to city in search of his prey.

In his own eyes, Saul was serving God. This troublesome new sect was disturbing the peace and threatening religious traditions. Yet his praiseworthy zeal had deteriorated into fanaticism and he was blinded to the possibility that he might actually be opposing God by opposing Jesus. Only a violent encounter with the truth could overwhelm such a violent adversary of the truth.

Saul hailed from the city of Tarsus in Asia Minor. Unlike the twelve, he hadn't witnessed the life, death, and resurrection of Christ, as the drama had played out in Judea and Galilee. The Christians' claims that Jesus had worked miracles, lived a sinless life, taught liberating truth, and risen from the dead after a tortured death were to him only false rumors, stories fabricated to lead astray the ignorant masses.

In fact, Saul was a Pharisee. No doubt he assumed that his fellow Pharisees at Jerusalem, nearly all of them implacable foes of

Jesus, held the correct views on the controversy. To shake him loose from such assumptions, God had to grant him the opportunity to become, like the others, an eyewitness of the risen Christ.

The Damascus Road

It happened on the road to Damascus, as he was "breathing threats and murder against the disciples of the Lord," on the way to round up more of them for jail (Acts 9:1). In an instant, Saul experienced his own version of the Transfiguration on the mountain. A light from heaven flashed about him, and a voice from heaven terrified him: "Saul, Saul, why do you persecute me?" (Acts 9:4). Knocked to the ground, blinded by the brilliance, he could not argue with the living God.

Jesus had appeared to all the others. Now he had appeared to Saul as well, "last of all, as to one untimely born," a babe among the apostles, but a witness no less (1 Cor 15:8). In the days following, he made up for lost time. The extraordinary energy he'd displayed as a Pharisee was focused now on the gospel of Christ. Traveling across the Roman world and establishing new churches wherever he went, he joined the other apostles in preaching, governing, working miracles, and suffering.

The persecutor became the persecuted, the predator the prey. In the years following, Paul—no longer called Saul—underwent a crash course in adversity: "Five times," he wrote his new converts, "I have received at the hands of the Jews the forty lashes less one. Three times I have been beaten with rods; once I was stoned. Three times I have been shipwrecked; a night and a day I have been adrift at sea; on frequent journeys, in danger from rivers, danger from robbers, danger from my own people, danger from Gentiles, danger in the city, danger in the wilderness, danger at sea, danger from false brethren; in toil and hardship, through many a sleepless night, in hunger and thirst, often without food, in cold and exposure" (2 Cor 11:24-27).

Paul knew as well as anyone that his work would lead sooner or later to his death. The Holy Spirit himself confirmed the fact one day when Paul stopped to minister in the town of Caesarea on the way to Jerusalem. A Christian prophet there took the apostle's belt, bound his own feet and hands, and warned: "So shall the Jews at Jerusalem bind the man who owns this girdle and deliver him into the hands of the Gentiles" (Acts 21:11).

Paul's friends and disciples begged him not to go on to Jerusalem. But, like Jesus, he had set his face toward the city, convinced that God was calling him to his destiny. "What are you doing," he asked them, "weeping and breaking my heart? For I am ready not only to be imprisoned but even to die at Jerusalem for the name of the Lord Jesus" (Acts 21:13).

On to Rome

Even so, Paul was not to die in Jerusalem. For a Jewish prophet, no other place would do for martyrdom (see Lk 13:33). But for a Roman citizen, the apostle to the nations, the final contest must be at Rome, the capital of the world.

The Christian brothers and sisters in the holy city welcomed him warmly. Their enemies lost no time in doing him violence. Rehearsing the familiar accusations that had roused the city against Stephen, they stirred the people to seize him and beat him, and would have killed him had the Romans not intervened. Taken into protective custody—the soldiers had to carry him aloft to keep him out of the reach of the frenzied mob—he nevertheless managed to win the ear of the tribune in charge.

The throngs fell silent when they realized that the tribune had allowed Paul to speak publicly. Bold like Stephen, he told them his story: his former hatred for the Church, his shattering encounter with the risen Christ, his commission to "be a witness for him to all men" of what he had seen and heard (Acts 22:15). Yet they couldn't bear the truth of his testimony, and they sought once more to kill him.

Once again Paul was spirited away from the developing riot. The following day brought a new round of imprisonment, threats, new opportunities to preach, and mob violence. That night he saw the Lord standing by him. Jesus said simply: "Take courage, for as you have testified about me at Jerusalem, so you must bear witness also at Rome" (Acts 23:11).

Meanwhile, more than forty of his adversaries had plotted together against him, swearing an oath that they would neither eat nor drink till they had killed him. The chief priests and elders joined them in arranging for an ambush, but a young man, Paul's nephew, uncovered the plan, and Paul was sent secretly to another town.

More days of prison, flight from his enemies, interrogations by Roman officials, well-reasoned defenses falling on deaf ears. Two years he was kept in limbo, till at last a new governor heard his case. His old enemies from Jerusalem came demanding that he be returned to their custody, giving them the chance for a new ambush. Yet Paul, a Roman citizen, demanded his legal right to bypass their maneuverings and appeal directly to Caesar. The governor agreed, and at last Paul set out by sea for Rome.

Months later, despite a storm and a shipwreck, he came to his destination and was placed under a rather lenient house arrest. The Roman Christians thrilled to welcome him. The Jewish leaders, curious but already prejudiced by evil slander against Jesus, invited him to tell his story. So he did—many times over the next two years, converting both Jews and Gentiles who came to his home.

Eventually Paul had his day before Caesar, but it was a Caesar demon possessed.

Nero

The emperor Nero had come to power through treachery and murder, and such wickedness remained the hallmark of his reign. For various reasons, he put to death his mother, his younger brother, his first wife, his second wife, and his unborn child—the last two when he kicked his pregnant wife in the belly. Countless others died brutally at his command. His court was a cesspool of sexual perversion and other vices; after murdering his second wife, he "married" a male youth who reminded him of her.

In the midsummer of A.D. 64, fire broke out in the crowded neighborhoods of Rome. Strong winds fanned the flames, devastating the city. The blaze continued for a week and left ten of the city's fourteen quarters in ashes.

Nero was at his seaside villa at the time. When he heard the news, he reportedly sang a song about the destruction of Troy, the city from whose citizens Rome had supposedly sprung. It was widely known that the emperor wanted to rebuild the center of the city and rename it for himself, so many quite reasonably believed that he himself had arranged to burn it down.

In any case, the emperor needed scapegoats. The Christians were a clever choice. Slanderous rumors already circulated about their religion; "everywhere," said the Roman Jews who debated Paul, "it [was] spoken against" (Acts 28:22). Adding to suspicions, the Christians tended to live in the poorer parts of town, which had somehow escaped the great fire. Perhaps most damning was the report that they believed the world would end in a conflagration.

Nero had multitudes arrested. A consummate sadist, he could hardly be satisfied with simple executions. Instead, he opened his gardens, with their chariot racecourse, to create a macabre spectacle. Mass crucifixions were the high point of the occasion, but other gruesome entertainment was arranged as well.

Christians were decked out in animal skins for mock hunts and thrown to hungry wild beasts. Others were forced to act in dramas whose plots led to their death. To light up the events at night, still others were covered with pitch and set afire as human torches.

"We glory," said Tertullian, a Christian writer of the following century, "in having such a man the leader in our punishment. For whoever knows him can understand that nothing was condemned by Nero unless it was something of great excellence."[4]

Paul was among those condemned to die. As a Roman citizen, he could be spared the outrages of Nero's gardens; he had the right to be beheaded outside the city walls instead. Thus the execution took place at the site now called Three Fountains—according to legends, so called because the water sprang up in each place where his severed head bounced.

Another witness had sealed his testimony in blood. Another athlete of God had won the contest. Paul had in fact written his own epitaph some days before: "I am already on the point of being sacrificed; the time of my departure has come. I have fought the good fight, I have finished the race, I have kept the faith. Henceforth there is laid up for me the crown of righteousness, which the Lord, the righteous judge, will award to me on that Day, and not only to me but also to all who have loved his appearing" (2 Tm 4:6-8).

St. Peter
Rock of the Martyrs

The other great pillar of the early Church, St. Peter, preached the gospel, as Paul did, in countless cities and villages. Ancient tradition places him in a variety of cities: Antioch, Syria, Cilicia,

Pontus, Galatia, Bithynia, Cappadocia, and other parts of Asia. But he, too, came at last to Rome, for he was the Rock upon which Jesus would build his Church (see Mt 16:18), and his Church was to be governed from Rome.

"Where Are You Going?"

A number of legends have come down to us about Peter's last days in the capital city: stories of a visit with a Roman senator's family, of a conflict with Simon the Magician (see Acts 8:9-24), of a daughter named Petronilla. Perhaps the most compelling story tells how, at the urging of the Christian community, he attempted to escape Nero's holocaust by fleeing the city. As he was hurrying out of town, he met Jesus on the road.

"Lord, where are you going?" he asked.

I am going to Rome to be crucified.

"Lord, weren't you crucified once for all?"

I saw you fleeing from death, and I wish to be crucified instead of you.

"Lord," said Peter, repenting, "I am going; I will fulfill your command."

Then fear not. For I am with you.

Peter was called, as Paul had been, to "complete what is lacking in Christ's afflictions for the sake of his body, that is, the church" (Col 1:24).

Crucified Head Down

The manner of Peter's death had, in fact, been prophesied long before by the Lord himself. After his resurrection, beside the sea, he had spoken to Peter about his last days.

When you are old, you will stretch out your hands, and another will gird you and carry you where you do not wish to go (Jn 21:18).

And so it was: In Nero's persecution, the Prince of the

Apostles was crucified, his hands stretched out to embrace the world as his Master's hands had been. He was pleased to imitate Jesus so closely in his death, yet humility demanded a holy distinction: In one last stroke of boldness, Peter asked to be nailed to the cross head down—a declaration that he was unworthy to die exactly as the Lord had died.

We cannot know what physical torments such an inversion may have added to his agony. Yet we can imagine that whatever the pain in his dying moments, the vision of Christ's Transfiguration so many years before remained in his soul, shimmering with hope and flooding his heart with courage. He had said as much in a letter to the churches. The memory of that "holy mountain," he wrote, where he had witnessed "the Majestic Glory," would serve as "a lamp shining in a dark place, until the day dawns and the morning star rises" (see 2 Pt 1:16-19).

So Peter gave up the ghost, and having conquered through him, his Lord gave him that promised morning star (see Rv 2:26-28). The Rock of the martyrs, made firm in grace, had fulfilled his own prophecy: "And after you have suffered a little while, the God of all grace, who has called you to his eternal glory in Christ, will himself restore, establish, and strengthen you" (1 Pt 5:10).

First death, then glory.

FOUR

"WE MUST OBEY GOD RATHER THAN MEN"
Martyrs Executed by the State

Whether it is right in the sight of God to listen to you rather than to God, you must judge; for we cannot but speak of what we have seen and heard.... We must obey God rather than men.

ACTS 4:19-20, 5:29

What have you to do with the kings of this world, in whom Christianity has never found anything save envy towards her?... A king persecuted the brethren of the Maccabees. A king also condemned the three youth to the sanctifying flames, being ignorant what he did, seeing that he himself was fighting against God. A king sought the life of the infant Savior. A king exposed Daniel, as he thought, to be eaten by wild beasts. And the Lord Christ himself was slain by a king's most wicked judge.

St. Augustine,
Answer to Letters of Petilian, 2, 93, 202

When Christians who survived the terrors of Nero read the Book of Revelation, no doubt they saw in St. John's description of the "Beast" a portrait of that brutal madman (see Rv 13:1-10). To late-first-century believers, the "mother of harlots and of earth's abominations ... drunk with the blood of the saints and the blood of the martyrs of Jesus," was no mystery: The "seven mountains" on which she was seated were obviously the seven hills of pagan Rome, the capital of the empire that so fiercely tormented them (Rv 17:5-6, 9).

Nevertheless, multiple interpretations of the vision were possible. John's revelation clearly had connections to other persecutions as well. His words often echoed, for example, passages of the ancient Hebrew prophet Daniel. Many Jews of the second century B.C., suffering torture and death for their faith under the foreign king Antiochus Epiphanes, no doubt had recognized that ruler's cruelties in Daniel's account of the fourth "beast," with its great horn that "made war with the saints" (see Dn 7:19-22). On the other hand, Jesus had explicitly cited Daniel's warnings when speaking of days yet to come (see Dn 11:31; Mt 24:15).

Did the scriptural prophecies of a ruler oppressing God's people speak, then, of Antiochus, or Nero, or someone in the future? Who exactly is the "Antichrist," as the Scripture calls him—the one literally "against Christ"—who persecutes the Church? St. John provides a clue in his first letter: "As you have heard that antichrist is coming, so now many antichrists have come.... Every spirit which does not confess Jesus is not of God. This is the spirit of antichrist, of which you heard that it was coming, and now it is in the world already" (1 Jn 2:18, 4:3).

Antichrist
The demonic power driving the Antichrist has been operating in the world since ancient times. The early Church fathers, and many Catholic writers since their day, have agreed that the end of time will see the most terrible persecution ever to ravish the Church, instigated by a godless political leader who is well portrayed by the divine revelations to Daniel and John, and well

deserving of the title *Antichrist*. They also have agreed that other antichrists will precede him as precursors, anticipating his wickedness. They are "shadows and forebodings, earnests and operating elements," as Cardinal John Newman called them, of the final great persecutor to come.

Thus, throughout the history of the Church, Christians have found in their own generations men who seemed to match the scriptural portrait of "the man of lawlessness ... the son of perdition" (2 Thes 2:3)—people deserving of the name Antichrist, heading governments or armies that inherited the anti-Christian spirit of Rome. Nero, Muhammed, the French revolutionaries, Hitler, Stalin, Mao—these and many others as well have initiated or inspired great political persecutions of the Church. In the twentieth century especially, when so much of the globe has been dominated by atheistic totalitarian regimes, the ranks of the martyrs John envisioned so long ago have swelled, "until the number of their fellow servants ... should be complete" (Rv 6:11).

A Clash of Kingdoms

Why has there so often been a conflict between Christians and their governments? In a day when people chant so glibly the mantra "separation of church and state," some may find it difficult to understand what all the controversy has been about. Politics is public, we're told; religion is private. If each keeps to its appropriate sphere of concern, we should avoid any conflict.

Yet even a moment of serious reflection reveals the naïveté of such platitudes. Any religion worthy of the name makes ultimate demands on behalf of Ultimate Reality—makes demands on every aspect of a believer's life, public as well as private, corporate as well as individual. When the state makes claims that contradict these demands of faith, the defiant words of the apostles to the authorities of their day echo once more: "We must obey God rather than men" (Acts 5:29).

Not surprisingly, then, we find that the Church in every age has produced martyrs who died giving "to Caesar the things that are Caesar's, and to God the things that are God's" (Mt 22:21). They drew a heroic line with their blood, a courageous boundary that said to the state: *Beyond this point you may not go.*

Jesus Versus the State

From the very beginning, state officials sensed that allegiance to Christ could compete with and even challenge allegiance to themselves and the political structures they represented. At our Lord's trial, the Roman governor Pilate cared little for Jewish theological arguments or the religious leaders' charges of blasphemy. He focused instead on whether Jesus did in fact see himself as "the King of the Jews," and what impetus that title might give to a revolt against Rome (see Jn 18:28–19:16).

Even when Pilate seemed satisfied that Jesus posed little military threat to the Roman occupation, public perceptions remained a problem. Once the crowds had screamed about Caesar's friends and enemies, the governor could hardly afford to ignore the imperial politics of the controversy.

The issue was power, pure and simple.

"Do you not know," boasted Pilate to Jesus, "that I have power to release you, and power to crucify you?"

"You would have no power over me," Jesus replied, "unless it had been given you from above" (Jn 19:10, 11).

The kingdoms of this world had run head-on into the kingdom of the next.

The Church and Pagan Rome

Ancient Rome could sometimes show itself hospitable to the alien religions it encountered as it expanded its borders through conquest. Traditionally polytheistic—that is, believing in multiple gods—pagan Romans had few reservations about adding a few exotic deities to their collection. Eminently practical, they were eager to do so if it made governing or doing business with their subject peoples a little easier.

Nevertheless, the upstart Christian God had a nasty habit of knocking the other gods off the altar. Pagans came to discover that this new *Christus* could not be content with a pinch of incense tossed his way as they went out to enjoy the public games in honor of native deities. Loyalty to Christ meant rejection of all other claims to divinity—including that of vain emperors who declared themselves worthy of worship.

A Strange Crowd

Christians appeared to their pagan neighbors as a strange crowd who acted suspiciously. After all, followers of the Nazarene stayed away from the civil ceremonies where all respectable citizens should have gathered, protesting that they couldn't approve of the religious aspects of the rites. They refused to burn incense to images of the emperors, because that act was tantamount to honoring the ruler as divine. While everyone else accepted without much thought the slogan "Caesar is lord," the Christians insisted instead, "Jesus is Lord." Yet this Jesus they worshipped was a rabble-rouser who had been executed by the Roman government for sedition!

No doubt about it: The followers of Jesus were troublemakers. They spoke against the celebrated gladiatorial games and the casual abandonment of unwanted infants to death or slavery. They resisted or even refused military service. Within their assemblies, everyone from senators to slaves was welcomed; whatever their social status, they embraced one another as spiritual equals. And they criticized popular practices such as astrology, divination, and the wearing of amulets.

In the eyes of a government anxious to maintain political control, any challenge to the social and religious status quo had to be crushed. Christians obviously showed disloyalty, even contempt, for Roman traditions and the vast empire those traditions helped to hold together. Worse yet, they met in secret, denying pagans entrance to their sacred "mysteries," as they called them. The rumors flew about what they might be seeking to conceal.

No doubt, they whispered, the Christians were holding wild orgies. And didn't they sometimes speak of eating someone's body and blood? Cannibalism! Didn't the women call their husbands "brother" and the men call their wives "sister"? Incest!

Atheists, the pagans called them—not because they believed in no god, but because they refused to recognize the Roman gods. Surely such irreverence was provoking the wrath of Jupiter and all the other traditional deities. Thus Christians were blamed for every disaster that came along. "If the Tiber floods, or if the Nile fails to flood," lamented Tertullian, "if the skies darken or the earth quakes, if famine, war or plague takes place, then immediately one shout goes up: 'The Christians to the lions! Death to the Christians!'"[1]

What St. Paul heard about Christians from first-century Romans became more emphatically true in the two centuries following: "With regard to this sect we know that everywhere it is spoken against" (Acts 28:22). Urged on by the suspicions, slander, and superstition of the pagan populace as a whole, the imperial government turned against the followers of the new religion as a threat to the security of the empire.

Imperial Terror

Just how severe persecution became depended largely on the whims of individual emperors and the various tempers of local populations. The terror was sometimes sustained, but more often sporadic. Even when universal decrees were issued against Christians throughout the empire, enforcement of the laws varied from region to region according to the policies of the local rulers. Waves of violence against the Church began with Nero's attack in A.D. 64 and continued, off and on, for three hundred years.

God alone knows how many thousands of believers perished. They were scourged, mutilated, beheaded, crucified; they were skinned and disemboweled while still alive; they were roasted on red-hot griddles or burned at the stake; they were thrown into the arena to be devoured by ravenous beasts or hacked to death by gladiators. Among those spared the death sentence, the men were typically enslaved for life in the nightmarish conditions of the lead mines, while the women were sold to brothels.

Hatred for the Christians knew no bounds. Punishments simply for confessing the name of Christ were wildly out of proportion to any crime they could possibly have committed. The same diabolical forces that had raged so cruelly against Jesus now drove those in power to fits of madness as they tortured and murdered his followers.

St. Polycarp of Smyrna

About the year A.D. 155 the demons grew restless in the city of Smyrna, a port on the central Aegean seacoast of Asia Minor. The Christians there were one of the "seven churches of Asia" Christ had addressed a generation before through St. John when he recorded the messages in the Book of Revelation (see Rv 1:11; 2:8-11). Even then our Lord had warned that the devil was plotting terrors against them (see Rv 2:9-10).

Polycarp, the aged bishop of the city, was revered as a spiritual leader throughout the Asian churches. Mentored by St. John the apostle himself, and having conversed with others who had walked with Jesus, Polycarp was confident of the sources of his faith. He served the Church as a courageous defender of Catholic orthodoxy, devoting much of his time to uprooting certain heresies that had sprung up like weeds in the young community.[2]

Holy Boldness

The old bishop was known for boldly speaking his mind. On a visit to Rome, Polycarp happened to meet up with the arch-heretic Marcion. Claiming to be Christian, Marcion had been leading astray many naïve believers with his fanciful tales of two gods, one evil and one good, the first the god of the Old Testament, the second the god of the New. Such teaching was spiritual poison.

With characteristic brashness, Marcion approached the august bishop and said curtly: "Do you recognize me, Polycarp?"

"Indeed," the feisty old saint replied. "I recognize you as the firstborn of Satan."

Soon after Polycarp returned home from Rome, the imperial officials at Smyrna held a pagan religious festival, marking the celebrations with the arrest of several prominent Christians of the city. Then the tortures began. "They were so torn with scourges," reported eyewitnesses, "that the frame of their bodies, even to the very inward veins and arteries, was laid open."

Yet much more was to come. If the prisoners refused to renounce Christ and offer an idolatrous sacrifice, macabre deaths awaited them. For the entertainment of the crowds, some were burned alive. Others were stretched out on beds of spikes. Still others were thrown to wild beasts.

A few faltered. One Christian named Quintus, visiting from Phrygia, though not sought out by the authorities, had insisted on presenting himself to them voluntarily for trial, pressuring a few others to do the same. When he saw the beasts, however, his rashness melted into terror, and the officials convinced him to apostasize.

Most, however, remained faithful. An elderly believer named Germanicus, threatened with being fed to a starving beast, set a stunning example for his fellow prisoners. When the Roman proconsul urged him to compromise his faith, he replied by walking out to meet the raging animal, deliberately attracting its attention and provoking it to devour him immediately. If he had to die for his Lord, then he would waste no time in doing so.

The mob was infuriated by his action. "Away with the atheists!" they screamed, thirsting for blood. "Find Polycarp!"

When the bishop first heard that the officials were seeking him, he resolved to stay in the city rather than flee. A number of his followers insisted that he leave, however, so he moved to a friend's house in the country not far away. There he spent day and night praying, as was his habit, for the Church and the world.

One day as he prayed he had a vision: The pillow under his head had burst into flames. Turning to his comrades, he said simply: "I am to be burned alive."

The Arrest

Three days later they came to arrest him. The soldiers found him lying down in an upper room with a way of escape that would have allowed him to flee again, had he been willing. But he had refused to run any farther, saying only, "The will of God be done."

When Polycarp heard that the soldiers had arrived, he came downstairs to talk with them. Showing his enemies gracious hospitality (and perhaps a touch of slyness), the bishop ordered the servants to bring them as much food and drink as they wished. Then he obtained their permission to pray undisturbed for an hour while they feasted.

His heart overflowed, not with petitions for himself, but with intercession for others. For two full hours as his captors listened, he stood praying for "all who had ever come in contact with him, both small and great, illustrious and obscure, as well as the whole Catholic Church throughout the world." Before he was done, some of the men began to regret their mission.

Nevertheless, the soldiers had their orders, so they set Polycarp on a donkey and brought him back to the city a prisoner. He was soon met by the irenarch—the title, ironically, means "peace official"—whose duty was to apprehend disturbers of the peace, such as these troublesome Christians. The man bore, appropriately, the accursed name of Herod.

He welcomed the elderly priest into his chariot and offered honeyed words to win him over. "What harm is there," Herod asked sweetly, "in saying, 'Caesar is lord,' and offering a little sacrifice, and taking part in the rituals, if it will assure your safety?"

Polycarp remained silent. When Herod persisted, however, he finally replied, "I will not do what you advise me to do." Once the irenarch had lost hope of persuading him, the pleasant mask came off. He flung bitter threats into the old man's face and shoved him roughly out of the chariot. Polycarp sprained his ankle in the fall, but remained undaunted, hobbling resolutely toward the stadium, where the mob roared so loudly that all other sound was drowned out.

The Trial

Yet God's voice could pierce even such deafening noise. As Polycarp entered the stadium, he and the other Christians around him heard words of divine encouragement from heaven ringing clearly above the din: *Be strong, and show yourself a man, Polycarp!* And so he did.

Word spread through the stands that the infamous ringleader of the Christians had arrived. The mob was shrieking deliriously now. Brought before Statius Quadratus, the Roman proconsul, Polycarp identified himself. The officer attempted, as Herod had, to persuade him to commit idolatry and condemn his Christian brothers and sisters. But the Roman hadn't counted on butting heads with the bull that was Polycarp.

"Have respect for your old age," Quadratus advised. "Swear by the fortune of Caesar. Repent and say, 'Away with the atheists!'"

Polycarp gazed sternly at the frenzied multitude in the stadium, waved his hand toward them, looked up to heaven and said bluntly, "Away with the atheists!"

The proconsul was not amused. Yet he could profit politically more by the bishop's apostasy than by his martyrdom, so he persisted. "Swear," he said, "and I will set you free. Condemn Christ."

The bishop now made himself perfectly clear. "Eighty-six years I have served him," he thundered, "and he has never done me wrong. How could I possibly blaspheme my King and my Savior?"

Still Quadratus pressed him. Polycarp continued his rebuke. "Since you pretend not to know who and what I am, let me tell you boldly: I am a Christian. And if you wish to hear what the teachings of Christianity are, appoint me a day, and you will hear them."

"Persuade the people," said the Roman glibly.

"To you I've thought it right to offer an account of my faith," replied the Christian. "For we're taught to give all due honor to the powers and authorities ordained by God, as long as that honor doesn't injure our souls. But as for this mob, I don't think they're worthy to judge my defense."

The proconsul hardened. "I have wild beasts waiting. If you don't repent, I'll throw you to them."

"Then call for them," said Polycarp. "We Christians aren't in the habit of repenting of what's good in order to embrace what's evil. If what you do allows me to trade my life in this evil world for life in the righteous world to come, then you do me a favor."

"So you think nothing of the wild beasts?" said Quadratus. "Then I'll burn you alive in the flames if you don't change your mind!"

The bishop remained unmoved. "You threaten me with fire that blazes only for an hour and then burns out. But you ignore the fire of the coming judgment and of eternal punishment that's reserved for the ungodly. What are you waiting for? Bring out against me whatever you wish."

The Execution

The proconsul was astounded by the old man's steel. Far from feeling terror, as the officials had expected, the bishop radiated joy as he was presented for execution. The herald was sent to the center of the stadium to proclaim three times: "Polycarp has confessed that he is a Christian!" The crowd went wild.

"This is the teacher of ungodliness!" "The father of the Christians!" "The overthrower of our gods!" "The one who's taught so many not to sacrifice to the gods or to worship them!"

Then they cried out to the superintendent of the festival to let loose a lion on him. But the beast-baiting events in the bloody games had already been completed, so they agreed instead that Polycarp should be burned alive. His prophetic vision would be fulfilled.

Not content only to watch, many from the stands rushed to gather firewood from the shops and public baths of the city. When the pyre was ready, Polycarp laid aside his clothes and stood on the faggots. Soldiers approached to nail him to the stake, the standard procedure for preventing criminals from attempting to escape the flames.

"Leave me as I am," he told them bluntly. "The One who gives me strength to endure the fire will also enable me to stand firm in the pyre without the help of your nails."

He put his hands behind his back so they could be bound. Then Polycarp looked up to heaven and prayed.

O Lord God almighty ... I give you thanks that you have counted me worthy of this day and of this hour, that I should have a part in the number of your martyrs, in the cup of your Christ, in order to be resurrected to eternal life, both of soul and body, through the immortality imparted by the Holy Spirit.... I praise you for all things, I bless you, I glorify you, along with ... your beloved Son, with whom, to you, and the Holy Spirit, be glory both now and to all coming ages. Amen!

If Polycarp felt grief, it was drowned by a flood of hope in Christ. With his last breath he offered not a lament but a grand doxology. His flock took careful note of how a true soldier of Christ should face death, and many of the pagans marveled as well.

As soon as he'd said "Amen," the fire was kindled. A massive blaze erupted, yet even then the ornery old saint continued his troublemaking. Eyewitnesses report that the flames suddenly bellowed out like wind-filled sails, burning all around him but leaving him untouched. "He appeared, not like flesh being consumed," they said, "but like bread baked in an oven, like gold and silver glowing in the furnace," and a sweet fragrance came from the pyre, "as if precious spices were smoking there."

There was nothing left for the executioners to do but to finish off Polycarp another way. One of them pierced him through with a dagger, and a torrent of blood poured out, extinguishing the flames. Some even reported that they saw a dove come forth from the wound.

A Seal on the Persecution

The bishop's grieving friends immediately begged the governor for permission to bury his remains, so that they could "have fellowship with his holy flesh," as they put it. Only a generation after the last of the apostles, already the Church had learned to venerate the relics of saints. But some officials present insisted that the request be denied. "Otherwise," they suggested cleverly, "these people might abandon the Crucified One and begin to worship this man instead."

That was merely an excuse for further malice, of course. "It's impossible," the Christians protested, "for us ever to forsake Christ ... or to worship anyone else. For we adore him as the Son of God; but the martyrs, as disciples and followers of the

Lord, we rightly love because of their unsurpassable affection toward their own King and Master—may we also be made fellow partakers and disciples of him!"

In the end, the bishop's body was thrown into the flames, and this time the flesh was consumed. Yet afterward a few brave souls took the bones that were left, "more precious than the most exquisite jewels, more tried than gold," and deposited them in a place of honor. Gathering there each year on the anniversary of his death, they celebrated his martyrdom, "both in memory of those who have already finished the race, and to exercise and prepare those who have yet to run in their steps."

The persecution soon waned; Polycarp's death, said his flock, had "put a seal" on it. St. John's prophecy for Smyrna had been fulfilled, as had Christ's promise to them: "Be faithful unto death, and I will give you the crown of life" (Rv 2:10). Convinced that an account of the bishop's martyrdom would encourage other churches, the Smyrnan Christians carefully recorded the events in detail and sent them out to believers in other cities.

In their confident declaration, we hear again the bold faith of their beloved bishop, echoing beyond the grave: "The blessed Polycarp suffered martyrdom.... He was taken by Herod ... Quadratus being proconsul—but Jesus Christ being King forever, to whom be glory, honor, majesty and an everlasting throne, from generation to generation. Amen!"

St. Perpetua

A generation later, and on another continent, the demons agitated once more. In the year 202 the Roman emperor Septimius Severus issued an edict outlawing all conversions to the Christian faith.

Catechumens and those responsible for their conversion were to receive the death penalty.

In northern Africa, persecution soon raged, especially at the great coastal city of Carthage, where the ancient, wicked Canaanite idols were still worshipped with human sacrifice. Now the dark gods haunted the city, demanding to be fed, and this time they lusted for the blood of two young mothers and their children.

Vibia Perpetua was a young African matron of noble birth, about twenty-two years old and liberally educated, married with an infant son not yet weaned. Defying the imperial edict, she and several companions had become Catholic catechumens, receiving instruction to prepare themselves for baptism. Among the others were Saturninus and Secundulus, and two slaves, Revocatus and Felicitas. The last of these was eight months with child at the time of their arrest. They were joined in prison by Saturus, their catechist.[3]

Imprisonment

Perpetua's passion story, taken from her own prison journal, begins after the catechumens' arrest but before they were thrown into prison—perhaps during a brief period of house arrest. Right away we meet her pitiful father; he had come to talk her out of this suicidal madness. When she remained adamant, the old man broke into a rage, but eventually left.

In those first days of their trial, the catechumens were baptized, and none too soon. Not long afterward, they were thrown into a wretched dungeon. Perpetua's humility shines through her admission of terror. "I was very much afraid," she wrote, "because I had never felt such darkness." The heat, the filth, the malice of the soldiers, the crowded cells all left her in shock. Worst of all, she feared for the life of her baby.

Two deacons from the local church bribed the guards to let the captives out for a few hours into a less oppressive part of the prison. Once out of the dungeon, they took what physical refreshment they could and Perpetua nursed her child, who by then was weak from hunger. The rest of her family—including her brother, who was himself a catechumen, though apparently undiscovered by the authorities—came to comfort her. Seeing their anguish, however, only intensified her own.

She entrusted the baby to the care of her relatives, but some days later she received permission to keep him with her in the dungeon. He became a little lamp in her darkness. "From that time on," she wrote, "I grew strong and was relieved from distress and anxiety about my infant; and the dungeon became like a palace to me, so that I preferred being there to being anywhere else."

A Vision of the Shepherd

At that time came the first of several visions the young woman received from heaven. One night in her sleep she saw a towering golden ladder, stretching up to heaven, yet so narrow that only one person could climb it at a time. Attached to the ladder's sides were swords, lances, hooks, daggers—iron weapons of every sort—so that anyone who climbed carelessly, or failed to look up in the climb, would be cut to pieces. Under the ladder crouched an immense dragon, lying in wait for those who climbed and trying to frighten them into abandoning the ascent.

Saturus climbed first, and when he reached the top, he called down to her: "Perpetua, I'm waiting for you; but be careful so the dragon doesn't bite you."

"In the name of the Lord Jesus," she said confidently, "he will not hurt me." Then, as she stepped on the first rung of the ladder, she stepped on the dragon's head as well.

When she reached the top, she found a vast garden, with a tall, white-haired Shepherd sitting there, milking sheep. Standing around him were thousands of martyrs in white robes. The Shepherd looked at her and said simply, "You are welcome here, daughter." Then he gave her a little cake of cheese, and as she ate it, the multitude around her said, "Amen."

At the sound of their voices she awoke, "still tasting a sweetness beyond description." She told her brother what she had dreamed, and they understood the meaning of it: She was to die. "From that time on," she noted, "we ceased to place any hope in this world."

Before the Tribunal

Soon word went out that the prisoners would be placed on trial. Perpetua's father visited her once more, worn out with anxiety, seeking some way to make her change her mind. "Have pity on my gray hairs!" he said, weeping. "With these hands I raised you to this flower of your age; I've even favored you over your brothers. Don't give me up to the scorn of men! Think of your brothers, think of your mother and your aunt—think of your son! He won't be able to live without you. Put aside your rashness. Don't bring us all to destruction—if you should suffer, then afterward none of us will be able even to speak freely."

He kissed her hands and threw himself at her feet. She was deeply moved, but she couldn't grant his request. So she did her best to comfort him. "On that scaffold," she said, "whatever God wills shall happen. For you must know that what we do is not in our own power, but in the power of God." He left her then, mourning all the more deeply.

A few days later they were called before the tribunal. A great crowd assembled to watch, with her father, who had managed to gain custody of her child, at the front. The other prisoners were interrogated and made their confessions. When it was Perpetua's turn, her father came up to her as she approached the steps to the scaffold, and said, "Have pity on your baby."

The procurator said to her: "Spare the gray hairs of your father; spare the infancy of your boy; offer sacrifice for the well-being of the emperor."

She remained adamant. "I will not."

"Are you, then, a Christian?"

"I am a Christian."

Then the procurator had her father cast down from the steps and beaten with rods. As she grieved for his injury, the sentence was passed: They would all be thrown to the wild beasts.

Perpetua sent one of the deacons to ask her father to return the child, but he refused. Nevertheless, she thanked God when she heard that the child, who had been nursing up until the time, no longer desired the breast; and from that time on her breasts no longer caused her any of the discomforts natural to a nursing mother.

The Final Days
In her final days, Perpetua's desperate father visited one last time. He threw himself face down on the ground, tore out his beard, "uttering words that would move all creation." Still he was unsuccessful, and as he left, Perpetua "grieved for his unhappy old age."

The day before the prisoners met their destiny in the amphitheater, Perpetua had one last dream. In it she saw herself enter the arena to fight, hand to hand, with a mighty opponent. After strenuous combat, she felled him and trod on his head.

Then a giant, dressed as a trainer of gladiators, awarded her a green branch bearing golden apples, kissed her, and said: "Daughter, peace be with you."

"Then I awoke," she wrote, concluding her journal, "and I understood that my combat was not with beasts, but with the devil."

Meanwhile, providential arrangements were being made for her fellow prisoners as well, each according to the destiny God had ordained. Secundulus died in the dungeon, and thus was spared the worst of the agonies. Felicitas had feared that her pregnancy would keep her from being executed with the others, since Roman law prevented her from being put to death until after she had given birth. The other Christians slated to die "were painfully saddened, lest they should leave so excellent a friend and companion to run the race of hope alone," so three days before the exhibition in the arena, they prayed fervently for the child to be born.

Immediately, Felicitas went into labor. As she groaned with the intense pains of childbirth, the jailers mocked her. "If you're suffering so much now," they taunted, "what will you do when you're thrown to the beasts—those same beasts you thought nothing of when you refused to sacrifice to Caesar?"

"What I suffer now, I suffer myself," she replied. "But then, there will be Someone else in me, who will suffer for me, because I, too, am about to suffer for him."

She gave birth to a daughter, and one of her Christian sisters took the child to raise as her own.

The Last Contest

The night before their exhibition, they ate together one last meal—the "free meal," the Romans called it, provided by the government as a token favor to those about to die. The

Christians declared it instead their *agape,* the brotherly "love feast" observed in the Church since the times of St. Paul (see 1 Cor 11:17-34). Strengthened by that feast, and by the firm solidarity it expressed, they prepared themselves for the final contest with the devil.

The next morning they woke to greet their day of victory. The gladiators of God walked to the amphitheater, "as if they were on their way to church," said the Christians watching, "full of joy, their faces brilliant." They were indeed on their way to meet their Lord—this time not in the Blessed Sacrament, but face to face.

Perpetua presented herself with great dignity, still the noblewoman, "a matron of Christ, beloved of God." Felicitas was thrilled that she had been safely brought forth, "from one bloodbath to another, from the midwife to the gladiator, to wash after childbirth with a second baptism." The others held their heads high and walked with a firm resolve.

As she approached the arena, Perpetua was heard singing. It was time, she knew, to chant psalms of thanksgiving. She was going home to the garden of the Shepherd, going out to tread on the devil and receive the victor's branch and kiss from the One who had prepared her for this day.

Revocatus, Saturninus, and Saturus addressed the crowds, warning them of the divine wrath to come. When they came before the procurator, the men gestured to him and shouted, "You judge us, but God will judge you!" For this last show of defiance, they were all run through a gauntlet of scourges. Despite the agony, the punishment brought them a special joy: Jesus had also been scourged; they clearly shared now in his passion.

Each prisoner was then sent out to face a wild beast; Perpetua was thrown to a wild heifer. It caught her on its horns and tossed her. As she lay bleeding, she noticed that her tunic had been torn from her side. "More mindful of modesty than suffering," as her Christian friends said, she pulled it over herself again. Her hair was disheveled, so she smoothed it into place—not out of vanity, but because unkempt hair was a sign of mourning, and she had no intention of entering glory looking sad.

Perpetua managed to stand up again and saw that Felicitas had been trampled by the cow. She went to her, gave her a hand, and lifted her to her feet. They stood together and were recalled to the gate. For a moment the brutality of the crowd was appeased—but only for a moment.

Two of the Christians still free found their way to them at the gate. Perpetua seemed as if she had just been awakened, "so deeply had she been in the Spirit and in an ecstasy." "I wonder," she said, looking around, "when we're to be led out to that heifer." They told her it had already happened, but she didn't believe it until she noticed that her tunic was torn and her body injured.

Then she knew her time had come. "Stand fast in the faith," she said to her fellows, "and love one another, all of you, and don't be scandalized by my sufferings."

The final act of the gruesome exhibition was to throw the victims into a pile and run each one through with a sword, to finish off any who might still survive. Those who could, stood up and moved to the place designated, but only after they had exchanged the traditional kiss of peace among Christian brothers and sisters. Then the swords were thrust into each one, and all but Perpetua at last lay dead.

She had been pierced between the ribs, but her valiant spirit lingered still. The young mother herself had to guide the wavering hand of the inexperienced gladiator to her throat for the final, mortal thrust. "Perhaps," said the Christian witnesses, "such a woman could not have been slain unless she herself had willed it—so fearful of her was the devil."

The Invasion of Islam

A few centuries slipped away, and Rome's judges were judged, its gods mocked or forgotten. Yet the martyrs of Carthage lived on in the communion of saints. The story of Perpetua, Felicitas, and the rest crossed the waters from North Africa into Europe, where the ancient victims of Rome were everywhere venerated and invoked by the Catholic faithful who came to populate what had been the Western empire.

In the seventh and eighth centuries, however, a new spiritual force came roaring out of the East, blazing its own path from North Africa into Spain. The followers of the fierce prophet Muhammed erupted from Arabia to conquer a vast collection of lands from Portugal to India, establishing the rule of his new religion, Islam, wherever they settled. In most of the vanquished lands, Christians who remained were subjected to special taxes and laws that sought to keep them separated from their conquerors as second-class citizens.

In an attempt to shield the new Muslim settlers from contact with the Christian faith, their rulers—sometimes known as *emirs*—destroyed churches and banned the construction of new ones. Even when Christians were able to preserve their buildings of worship, they often were forbidden to repair them. The emirs also frequently outlawed or restricted the ringing of church bells and the holding of public processions, including funerals.

Edicts discriminated against Christians on the social and political levels as well. Muslim women were forbidden to marry Christian men, and the children of religiously mixed marriages had to be raised as Muslims. Christians were forbidden to exercise authority over Muslims, so many political offices were closed to them. Any slave serving a Christian master could gain freedom simply by converting to Islam. Christians were sometimes required to wear special attire that identified their religion, and they were often forbidden to imitate the clothing and even the hairstyles of their Muslim neighbors. Christians' use of arms and saddles were also strictly limited.

Perhaps the most troublesome, and most severe, of the Muslim laws were the edicts against Christian evangelism, the conversion of a Muslim to Christian faith, and the public utterance of anything that could be considered "blasphemy" to Muslim ears. All of these actions might be punished by death. Laws against blasphemous speech were particularly broad, decreeing as a crime any criticism of the prophet Muhammed or denial of the truth of his teachings.

The Teachings of Islam

Islam, like Christianity, professes a single, divine Creator whose will must be obeyed and who has revealed himself through prophets who have spoken for him. Muslims even insist that this Allah, as they call him, is the same God worshipped by the Jews and Christians. Though Muhammed was the last and greatest of Allah's prophets, they believe, Jesus was also a prophet, born to Mary, a virgin.

Beyond these theological parallels, however, Muslim and Christian teachings differ radically. Muhammed denied the two most distinctive doctrines of Christian faith: that God is a Trinity of three Persons in one Being, and that the man Jesus Christ is God himself, the Second Person of the Trinity incarnate. Thus faithful Christians had to conclude that the prophet of Islam was in grave error about these matters, that his revelations were not divinely inspired, and that his followers had been misled.

Given these differences, the spiritual quandary faced by Christians under the Muslim laws becomes clear. To their credit, Muslims rarely forced Christians to convert to Islam at the point of a sword, allowing them to practice quietly in private if they paid their taxes and obeyed the other laws. Nevertheless, because the Christian faith is in its essence not a merely "private" faith, the rulers forced Christians to make a difficult choice.

On the one hand, they could remain silent around their Muslim neighbors about certain issues of ultimate importance— truths about the way to eternal life with God—knowing that those neighbors were in error and in danger of final damnation. They could turn away Muslims seeking Christian religious instruction. On the other hand, the Christians could speak openly about Christ—and forfeit their lives.

Sharpening the dilemma was the fact that the Christian faith, unlike some others, is by nature a missionary faith. Most varieties of Hinduism, for example, don't obligate followers to try to win non-Hindus to their religious point of view. But Christ himself, to whom all Christians owe full obedience, commanded his followers to preach his gospel, to bear witness to the truth of who he is and how he has made eternal salvation possible.

To remain perpetually silent about Christ, then, was not only to fail to testify to the truth, but to disobey the Lord. For priests to refuse catechetical instruction and baptism to those who sought it was to betray their vows. Not surprisingly, at least a few Catholics under Muslim domination found such a silence untenable.

At the same time, Muslims who wished to learn about Christianity, and especially those who wished to become Christians, faced their own terrible dilemma. On the one hand, they could deceive their families, their friends, and the authorities, with the inevitable compromises and anguish involved in such deceit. They could pretend sincerity when they attended religious services at the mosque, prayed publicly to Allah five times a day, and kept the other requirements of Muslim practice. Meanwhile, since going to church would give them away, "secret Christians" couldn't perform even that most basic of Christian acts.

On the other hand, secret Christians or Muslims seeking Christ could declare themselves openly—and die. A number of them ultimately chose to do so; "closet Christianity," they concluded, was a contradiction in terms.[4]

Muslim-Christian Cordoba

Cordoba, a city in southern Spain on the Guadalquivir River, fell to Muslim forces in 711. Though surviving legal records from that time are scanty, the Christians who didn't flee the city apparently submitted, however reluctantly, to the typical arrangements offered by Muslim conquerors: a heavy tribute, destruction or seizure of at least some church buildings, and various restrictions on the practice of their faith.

Within a few generations, the Cordoban Christians as a whole had worked out the kinds of uneasy accommodations typical in Christian lands that had been subdued by Islam. They sacrificed to scrape together the monthly tax. They made do with the church buildings left to them. They kept their liturgies low-key and indoors, and they made sure that funeral processions stayed out of Muslim neighborhoods. Most of all, whenever in public, they held their theological tongues.

In the meantime, enforcement of many anti-Christian laws had grown lax. Clothing legislation was tedious to implement. Church bells rang regularly again, if not too loudly. The emirs recruited Christians for their administrative bureaucracies, granting them at least a measure of influence, if not genuine power. Even bishops and priests sometimes aligned themselves closely with the ruler as his ministers, acting as his spokesmen and advisors for controlling the Christian community.

As usual in such settings, interfaith friendships emerged. These led as well—perhaps inevitably—to intermarriage between Muslims and Christians, uniting families across religious boundaries. Since peace provided the best climate for business, the commercial elite of the city, both Muslim and Christian, frowned on any behavior that might lead to religious conflict.

Yet, despite the religious truce, tensions bubbled beneath the surface. Muslims complained that Christians were allowed to serve as bureaucrats and even soldiers; sometimes they managed to have them fired. Irritated by the church bells, the followers of Muhammed would often try to drown out the ringing with loud curses. Priests, identifiable on the streets by their distinctive garb, were frequently taunted by Muslim children and even pelted with rocks and dung.

The status quo may have kept the peace politically and economically, but spiritual conditions were a different matter. In a milieu of pragmatic compromise, many souls grew lukewarm. Some Christians even apostasized and declared themselves Muslim. A few of these, perhaps, had found themselves too severely tempted by the prospect of freedom from the tax, or the lure of political advancement, or the relief of casting off second-class status. Others had succumbed through immersion in a culture that constantly denigrated their faith yet allowed it no public defense.

The Martyrs of Cordoba

In this adverse setting there appeared in the middle of the ninth century a number of Christians who decided at last to speak the truth about God, and to do it publicly. Our knowledge of their circumstances is rather limited. Only one of them left behind any account of the events surrounding the martyrdoms that resulted.

This believer, a priest and abbot named Eulogius, wasn't the first to die, and he certainly wasn't the most courageous among them. At one point he even fled the city to avoid trouble. Yet he figures largely in the martyrs' story because his cultured background gave him the literary and rhetorical skills to chronicle their sacrifices, to encourage their witness, and to serve as their apologist.[5]

Why did they need an apologist? In the delicate social and political climate of ninth-century Cordoba, many Christians apparently subscribed to a medieval version of "the Gospel of Nice." They sought to avoid offending their Muslim neighbors at all costs.

We must not judge them too harshly, considering that they faced death for speaking freely about their faith. Yet their sharp criticism of the martyrdoms suggests that they failed miserably to appreciate the genuinely evangelical grounds for such actions. Instead, they despised and ridiculed those who dared to threaten a status quo that allowed them to remain precariously safe, if shackled.

Perfectus

One incident that provoked local Christians to recognize more painfully the injustice of the blasphemy laws took place in the spring of the year 850. One day a local priest named Perfectus was stopped by a group of Muslims on his way to the market. Recognizing him as a priest by his clerical garb, they asked him to tell them what he believed about Christ and Muhammed.

Knowing that priests were often harassed, he sensed a setup and declined. Yet they persisted and swore to protect him from any legal consequences resulting from what he said. Taking them at their word, Perfectus then spoke forthrightly: Muhammed, he told them in Arabic, was one of the false prophets predicted by Christ, an immoral man who had seduced the wife of a kinsman.

His listeners were infuriated by what he said, but they kept their word and let him go on to the market. Yet, a few days later, when he encountered the same group, they had changed their minds, concluding that they no longer had to keep their oath. They seized the priest, took him before the magistrate, and testified against him. He was imprisoned, and on April 18, beheaded.

The Catholic community was outraged. No doubt at least a few of them began to think deeply in the following months about whether a public testimony to Christ might have become necessary: not only as a protest, but perhaps even as a provocation, so that their Muslim neighbors might be prompted to consider why someone would make such a sacrifice. More than a year passed, but in the summer of the next year a new incident shook the peace of the city.

Isaac and Others

Isaac, a well-educated Cordoban Catholic of noble birth, had risen to a high position within the local Muslim bureaucracy. Yet God had called him elsewhere: Eventually he'd left that post and retired to the monastery of Tabanos in the mountains north of the city, where he'd lived for three years. In the first week of June, 851, Isaac returned to Cordoba, walked to the palace of the emir—his former employer—and asked to see the judge.

When the judge appeared, Isaac asked him to discuss Islam. Once the judge began talking about the life of Muhammed, the monk responded with much the same forthright critique of the prophet that Perfectus had offered. Muhammed, he said, had misled his people and was now in hell.

The judge and his counselors were so taken back at his boldness that they suggested he must be drunk or crazy. But Isaac said no; "the zeal of righteousness" had pressed him to speak against Muhammed's errors publicly. He was ready to give his life for his witness.

The monk was arrested and sentenced to die for the crime of blasphemy. On June 3, he was beheaded and hanged upside down on the banks of the river for the rest of the Christians to see and fear. Then his body was burned and the ashes dumped in the water.

The authorities recognized the potential for trouble. Might the monk's example spur other rash men to follow? A new edict was issued, affirming the death penalty for publicly dishonoring the prophet.

Two days later, the scene was repeated. Sanctius, a young Christian soldier, had been born in France but captured by Muslim troops as a boy and raised to serve in the army of Cordoba. He appeared before the judge at the palace—he may, in fact, have served in the palace guard—and made his confession. He was also beheaded.

In the weeks to come the roll of the martyrs continued to grow, with priests, deacons, and monks coming forward to bear testimony. "We abide by the same confession," they declared to the judge, "that was professed by our most holy brothers Isaac and Sanctius. Now pass sentence, add to your brutalities, be fired with great wrath to avenge your prophet. We profess Christ to be truly God and your prophet to be a precursor of Antichrist, an author of profane teachings." All were executed without delay.

Flora and Maria

The next to die were Flora and Maria, the first of nine women to come forward. Maria, a nun, was the sister of another martyr, Walabonsus, whose death had touched her deeply. Maria had met Flora while praying for guidance in the church where Perfectus had served as priest.

Both Flora and Maria had been raised by parents in religiously mixed marriages. Maria's family had years before been forced to flee their country estate because of her Muslim mother's conversion to her father's Christian faith. Flora, on the other hand, should have been raised Muslim, according to the law, having had a Muslim father. But he'd died when she was still quite young, and she'd followed her mother's faith instead—though keeping it a secret from her Muslim brother.

In the end, Flora had run away from home to try to avoid the difficult situation. However, her brother, who must have been a man of some influence in Cordoba, was able to pressure the Catholic community there to compel her to return. He offered to reward her if she became Muslim, but to no avail; he roared threats, but still she was adamant that she would remain a Christian. He then brought her to the authorities.

There she was joined by Maria. Like the others who had come forward, Maria was executed for blasphemy. Yet Flora was a special case: Technically, she was considered not a blasphemer, but an apostate. She protested that she'd been a Christian since childhood, so she wasn't truly an apostate and was thus innocent of those charges. The judge responded by having her severely lashed and placed on probation under the custody of her brother. Though she eventually escaped from his home, she decided to return and die for her faith.

Scores of other Christians offered themselves to the authorities for execution in the months and years to come: priests and deacons, monks and laypeople, consecrated virgins and matrons, young and elderly. Between 850 and 859, a total of forty-eight believers were beheaded for offenses against the prophet.

Eulogius and Leocritia

Eulogius carefully chronicled all these martyrdoms and many others through the year 857. His responsibilities as priest and abbot left him little time to write. He found more opportunity to do so, however, when the emir threw most of the local Christian clergy into prison as a way of exerting pressure on the community to discourage potential martyrs.

Ultimately, Eulogius chose martyrdom himself by choosing to aid and encourage the others. His support for them had already brought him under the suspicion of the authorities and alienated him from Christians who sought to suppress the witnesses. The incident that brought matters to a head involved a young Muslim woman, Leocritia, who had been persuaded of the truth of the gospel.

Leocritia's secret conversion was discovered by her parents, and when they tried unsuccessfully to change her mind, she feared that her situation had become dangerous, spiritually and otherwise. She sought the advice of Eulogius and his sister through messengers. Both advised her to leave home, and they helped her plot the escape.

The family had officials search for the woman, at first unsuccessfully; Eulogius helped her find a series of hideouts and provided her catechetical instruction in the meantime. Eventually someone betrayed them to the authorities. Both were arrested: Leocritia for converting to the Christian faith, Eulogius for evangelizing her.

In his defense, the priest declared before the judge: "We have been ordained to preach, and by the nature of our faith we must spread its light to those who seek it from us. We must refuse no one who hastens along the paths of life that are holy. This is fitting for priests. This is what the true religion requires. This is what Christ our Lord has taught us.... So it was appropriate that I, as far as I was able, instruct, teach and present the faith of Christ as the way to the heavenly kingdom."

Eulogius ended his defense with an invitation. "I would be most eager to do the same for you," he said to judge, "if you should seek the same help from me."

The judge responded by having Eulogius scourged. Still the priest pressed on. Telling the judge that he might as well go ahead and sharpen his sword, Eulogius preached a brief homily on the truths of the Christian faith and the errors of Islam.

Royal counselors to the emir begged Eulogius to relent, but he refused. He was beheaded on March 11, 859, and Leocritia met the same fate three days later.

No doubt both the emir and a number of Cordoban Catholics breathed a sigh of relief to have the "instigator" of the troublemakers, as they called him, silent at last. Yet, inspired by their example, a trickle of public witnesses to Christ continued to meet their deaths in the city, even into the tenth century.

St. Pelagius

One of these, St. Pelagius, deserves special mention because of his youth. Pelagius was born in northern Spain about the year 912, just a generation after the events that led to the multiple martyrdoms to the south in Cordoba. When he was ten, his uncle, Bishop Hermogius of Tuy, was captured in a skirmish between Christian and Muslim forces. The boy's father, a Galician nobleman, sent Pelagius to the court of Abd ar-Rahman III, the Muslim caliph who resided in Cordoba, as a hostage in exchange for his uncle's release.

The boy remained a captive for three and a half years. During his captivity, the caliph repeatedly made him an offer: If Pelagius would convert to Islam and submit to the ruler's sexual advances, he would be guaranteed a life of freedom, wealth, and pleasure.

Each time, Pelagius refused. Eventually the caliph turned to threats instead. Still the boy remained firm. He was therefore tortured with red-hot tongs, and his right arm was cut off. Despite six hours of such torments, however, he clung to his faith and his purity, and was finally executed on June 26, 925.

A few years later, a German Benedictine poetess, Roswitha of Gandersheim, heard of the young saint from eyewitnesses who brought news of his death from Cordoba. She wrote a celebrated poem telling his story, thus guaranteeing that his example of courage and integrity would inspire young people for generations to come.[6]

We could hardly imagine a more diverse collection of individuals than the martyrs of Cordoba: men and women; children, middle-aged adults, and the elderly; priests, deacons, monks, nuns, and laypeople; married couples and singles; nobles and peasants; soldiers and scholars; Arabs and Spaniards;

converts and cradle Catholics. The circumstances under which they were arrested and condemned differed widely as well. Some preached publicly; some were "secret Christians" unwilling to continue living a lie; others simply appeared before the judge to testify solemnly that Jesus was God and Muhammed was a false prophet.

Despite such differences, however, they had one heroic trait in common: All of them bore witness by their deaths that they shared the faith of the apostles—who, when ordered not to speak publicly of Jesus, had replied simply, "We must obey God rather than men" (Acts 5:29).

FIVE

"THE OVERTHROWER OF OUR GODS"
Martyrs of the Mission Fields

*They dragged ... some of the brethren before the city authori-
ties, crying, "These men who have turned the world upside
down have come here also ... saying that there is another king,
Jesus." And the people and the city authorities were disturbed
when they heard this.*

ACTS 17:6-8

*Christianity is not a private way of salvation and a guide to
a pious life; it is a way of world salvation and a philosophy of
total life. This makes it a sort of dynamite. So when you send
missioners out to preach it, it is well to get ready for some
explosions.*

Bishop James Edward Walsh

The raging mob that filled the stadium at ancient Smyrna,
shrieking for the death of St. Polycarp as the "overthrower"
of their gods, provides a vivid reminder that not all his enemies
were agents of the state. Wherever the Christians showed up
with their strange new crucified God, they "turned the world
upside down," as the pagan Thessalonians put it (Acts 17:6).
The resulting turmoil eventually disturbed every segment of
society—male and female, young and old, rich and poor, slave
and free, ruler and subject. Once the shadow of the cross fell
over a people, things would never be the same again.

All human beings, St. Paul tells us, have access through nature itself to a certain awareness of God and his will. Yet ever since our first parents turned their backs on him, that truth has been obscured (see Rom 1:18-32). In fact, St. Paul insists, our race has actively *suppressed* that truth (v. 18). Countless human societies have thus been built on lies instead—each one a massive, complex edifice perched precariously on fickle, shifting sand (see Mt 7:26).

When Truth himself erupts on the horizon, then, the social results can be seismic, a cultural earthquake. Idols begin to tumble from their lofty temples. Cracks appear in the ancient highways of tradition. Every structure built on a false moral or spiritual foundation, however handsomely constructed, trembles and threatens to come crashing down.

Not surprisingly, people who feel their world falling apart around them react with anger, fear, and even hatred. The chasms opening up beneath them must be filled in again, filled with the corpses of those who have offended their gods and brought down on them all such a curse.

Thus the mission fields are planted thoroughly with martyrs, their blood-seed scattered from Palestine to Paraguay, from Georgia to Japan, from the Ukraine to Uganda.

St. Justin the Philosopher

We've already seen how the evangelistic efforts of the apostles and their disciples jolted the cities where they preached. In Ephesus, for example—the site of the massive temple of Artemis (or Diana), one of the seven wonders of the ancient world— Paul and his little missionary band came preaching in the streets, synagogues, and public halls, healing and casting out demons from the possessed. The result, reports St. Luke in his understated style, was "no little stir" (Acts 19:23).

New believers who had practiced sorcery confessed, gathered together their books of magical incantations in a great heap, and burned them publicly. Sales of silver shrines of the goddess Artemis fell dramatically, rousing the ire of that considerable segment of the business community which depended for its livelihood on the popularity of her cult. If enough people were persuaded by St. Paul's argument that "gods made with hands are not gods," her worshippers feared, "the temple of the great goddess Artemis may count for nothing, and ... she may even be deposed from her magnificence" (Acts 19:26-27).

Should we be surprised, then, that the coming of the Christians led some of the Ephesian people to riot? After all, their fears turned out to be fully justified. The goddess, the silver idols, the books of sorcery were ultimately forgotten, and the cross was raised above the new churches of that great city.

Even so, such a remarkable transformation of a culture didn't happen overnight. Nor were ordained preachers the only missionaries who accomplished the overthrow of the pagan gods. Then as now, the most fruitful mission fields were often those in which Christians of various secular occupations presented the gospel to their colleagues. In those days, however, speaking of Christ in even that setting could lead to death.

Accounts have survived that tell of such heroism by laymen and women. St. Andrew the tribune, for example, was a third-century soldier in the Roman imperial army stationed in Syria. The details of his story as we have it now may not be reliable, but the main outline seems clear: Andrew's commanding officer, Antiochus, hated the Church and had a history of executing Christian soldiers for their faith. Nevertheless, Andrew shared the gospel with the men who served under him, and most of the men became Christians. In the end, they were all slaughtered by Antiochus for bearing testimony to their faith.

A more detailed, and more reliable, account of heroic lay witness comes to us from the second century. St. Justin Martyr has been called the father of Christian literature and its first major apologist. His writings, great historical treasures preserved by the Church, supply us with considerable information about his life. The martyr's contemporaries recorded the events surrounding his martyrdom.[1]

A Pagan Samaritan Convert

Jesus converted a number of Samaritans in the village near Jacob's well (see Jn 4:1-42). The religious background of these converts was a variant of Judaism; they believed in the God of Abraham and expected the Messiah to come. Yet many residents of Samaria were pagan, polytheistic Greco-Romans who had settled there, and among these was St. Justin, born not long after the year A.D. 100.

No doubt his parents were people of some means, for Justin was well educated and traveled extensively. Taking up philosophy as his chief interest, he examined all the intellectual options popular at that time in Hellenistic culture, concluding that the Greek philosopher Plato offered the best understanding of the world. Nevertheless, Justin's heart and mind remained restless. He'd thought that philosophy would lead to happiness, but something was missing in even the best Greek philosophy.

One day Justin met a mysterious old man on the beach where he often walked to meditate. The man engaged him in a lively philosophical dialogue that introduced him to the Old Testament prophets and to the Good News about Jesus Christ. Then he walked away, and Justin never saw him again. "But right away a flame was kindled in my soul," the young philosopher later wrote. "A love of the prophets, and of those men who are friends of Christ, possessed me; and while turning his words over in my mind, I found this philosophy [of Christ] alone to be safe and of benefit."

The First Great Christian Apologist

Justin turned away abruptly from those aspects of pagan Greek thought that were contrary to the gospel. Yet he continued to wear the traditional philosopher's gown as the distinctive uniform of his profession. The term "philosophy," after all, meant literally "love of wisdom," and he now had fallen in love with Wisdom himself.

"Philosophy," wrote Justin, "is the knowledge of what really exists, and a clear perception of the truth." Anxious to persuade others of the truth he'd discovered, Justin soon turned his formidable intellectual powers to the service of the Church. With careful and powerful arguments, he began writing books to explain and defend the Christian faith to his fellow philosophers and to any educated people of the pagan culture who would listen.

Justin minced no words when he scrutinized the gods of the Greeks and Romans, known for their capricious and immoral behavior. "We—who out of every race of men, used to worship Bacchus ... and Apollo (who in their loves with men did things too shameful even to mention), and Proserpine and Venus (who were maddened with lust) ... or some one or other of those who are called gods—have now, through Jesus Christ, learned to despise these, even though we're threatened with death for doing so. Instead, we have dedicated ourselves to the unbegotten God, without human passions, who has never been goaded by lust." The pagan gods, Justin declared, were "wicked and impious demons."

At the same time, he confronted the malicious rumors about

Christians so prevalent in his society. Justin defended Christian moral standards, showing how superior they were to those of pagan culture, and explained Christian sacraments. He even described certain aspects of the Mass to allay fears that believers were engaging in orgies and cannibalism behind closed doors: "This food is called among us the Eucharist, of which no one is allowed to partake except those who believe that the things we teach are true.... We have been taught that the food which is blessed by the prayer of Christ's word ... is the flesh and blood of that Jesus who was himself made flesh."

Justin was as bold as he was brilliant. Since the Roman imperial government was launching erratic attacks on the Church, he decided that the emperor himself needed to hear the truth about Christ and his people. So Justin wrote two "apologies"—that is, defenses of the faith—addressed to the emperor Antoninus, to the Senate of Rome, to certain intellectuals close to the emperor, and to the Roman people as a whole.

To call attention to himself in this way no doubt brought considerable danger. The Roman despot could have had him beheaded on a moment's notice. "But it is incumbent on the lover of truth," Justin told the emperor, "by every means possible, to choose to do and say what is right. Even if threatened with death, he must choose truth over his own life."

If the members of the Roman court, Justin insisted, were truly "guardians of justice and lovers of wisdom," as they claimed to be, they wouldn't act upon mere rumors or the whims of "superstitious men." Instead, they would pass judgment only after a fair investigation of the truth. And what if the rulers condemned Justin and his fellow Christians unjustly? "No evil can be done to us," he concluded, confident of their heavenly destination and reward. "You can kill us, but you cannot harm us."

Trial and Martyrdom

This intrepid Christian philosopher traveled about the empire, debating with pagan philosophers, urging them to embrace divine Wisdom by believing the gospel. Eventually he came to Rome, where he founded a school of philosophers and taught his students about Christ. While there, Justin bested in debate a philosopher of the school of the Cynics named Crescens. (The name "Cynics" meant "dogs"; they were often known for their shamelessness.)

Embittered, Crescens sought a way to avenge himself on the man whose wisdom had shown him to be a fool. Apparently at the Cynic's instigation, during a season of intensified persecution of the Church about the year 165, Justin was denounced to the authorities and arrested. Along with several companions, he was commanded by the Roman prefect to choose between worshipping the pagan gods or execution. Justin attempted briefly to tell the officials present about the truth of Christian teachings, but they refused to be moved.

"Unless you obey us, you will be punished without mercy," said the prefect.

"Do whatever you will," said the prisoners, "for we are Christians, and we do not sacrifice to idols."

They were led away to be scourged and beheaded. Yet the philosopher and his friends met their deaths with a firm hope. "Do you really suppose," the prefect had asked with a sneer, "that you will ascend to heaven to receive a reward?"

"No, I don't suppose it," replied Justin. "Rather, I know it and I am fully persuaded of it."[2]

St. Boniface
Apostle of Germany

Nearly six centuries later, Rome's emperors were dust. Yet the gospel continued to shake the world, finding its way into the deep forests of northern and central Europe for a confrontation with those the Romans had called "barbarians." These people, too, believed in many gods. Unlike the deities of Rome and Greece, however, their gods lusted less for boys than for battle.

The chieftains who worshipped these gods tended to be preoccupied with predatory warfare and the tribute it could win for them. Meanwhile, superstition pressed the common people to sacrifice to the lesser nature spirits and to seek supernatural help in more mundane affairs, such as health, livelihood, and social relations. For these needs they often sought out the *ariolus*—what today might be called a witch doctor or shaman—for the work of augury, soothsaying, divination, and magic.

The parallels with the situation St. Paul found in ancient Ephesus are clear, and the coming of the gospel would be just as explosive. All it took was a daring Christian missionary with the courage to challenge the old gods directly—a man such as St. Boniface. One episode from his evangelistic career will illustrate.[3]

Showdown at the Sacred Oak

Rumors ran like wildfire through the little German village of Geismar: Boniface, that troublesome English foreigner, was headed for the shrine of the gods, axe in hand, to fell the mighty sacred oak.

For some time now he'd preached to the people of the surrounding district of Hesse, urging them to forsake the gods of their fathers for the one true God who had created the world. Many had believed his message and been liberated from the bondage of their superstitions.

Others, however, had insisted that adopting the new Roman religion was a dangerous course to take. The ancient tribal deities would be offended if they were deserted. The people would lose the gods' protection, and their indispensable aid in battle would be withdrawn. Sickness would plague them, and there would be no remedy. The very trees and springs would turn against them.

A great, angry crowd of those who opposed the new faith gathered at the shrine, and they found that the rumors were true. Boniface, the fiery Englishman, the bold Christian bishop, stood before the towering oak with his axe, surrounded by his priests and converts. The pagans cursed him bitterly.

Some of them thought to rush upon him and put an end to this nonsense once and for all, but others objected. Let the gods themselves deal with this foreigner, they said. Step back and watch the divine thunderbolts fall from the sky to burn up the Christians and protect the sacred tree.

Boniface took up his axe and began to chop. The trunk was massive; with one man cutting, the task could take all day. After only a few blows of the axe, however, a sudden wind came up. The bishop ceased his labor and watched as the blast of air seemed to focus all its energy on the tree, pressing against the great branches until the sound of their cracking could be heard. No more curses now; the crowd fell silent.

At last the trunk itself began to groan, resisting the wind, but in the end the wood was vanquished. The sacred oak came crashing down. When it hit the earth, it split into four pieces— making fine lumber, decided Boniface, for building a small chapel where Christ could be worshipped on that very spot.

The church was built and dedicated to St. Peter, and in the days to come many of those who had cursed the bishop and his axe came to the church to be baptized. The haughty, bloody gods of their fathers had been defeated. The God of Boniface was Lord.

Early Life

Who was this brash Englishman, and how had he come to preach in Germany?

Born in Wessex around the year 680, Wynfrith—his English name—early on showed a sharp interest in religion. Even when he was only five, according to his disciple and first biographer, St. Willibald, "his chief delight was to hear holy men converse about God and heavenly things." Some monks on a preaching mission in his area once came to his father's house, and he was so deeply impressed by their words that he decided to enter the religious life as well.

The youth's father firmly opposed such plans and refused to grant him permission to pursue them. However, a serious illness threatened the older man's life, and caused him to relent, concluding that God was chastising him for his opposition to the boy's vocation. At the age of thirteen, then, Wynfrith entered the monastery school at Exeter to study grammar and begin a life of ascetic discipline even before he took his vows.

Having at last become a monk after several years of study, Wynfrith went on to a second monastery, this one in Winchester, to continue his studies in the classical curriculum of the day: poetry, rhetoric, history, and the Scriptures. He excelled so highly as a scholar that eventually the abbot appointed him to teach these subjects. Once ordained at age thirty, he began to preach and care for the souls of the neighboring parishes. His fame as a preacher and teacher grew until soon the bishops of the region were inviting him to their synods to serve as a theologian and counselor.

Missionary Labors

Nevertheless, Wynfrith's heart was set on the mission field. He received from his abbot permission to go preach to the Frisians (in what is now Holland), but a civil war prevented the mission from succeeding. Not long after he'd returned to his monastery, his abbot died, and he was unanimously chosen as successor. Protesting that his true vocation was to convert the pagans, he accepted the position but soon convinced the monks to replace him so he could be free to evangelize.

In 719, the priest set out for Rome, equipped with a letter of commendation from his bishop, to seek the apostolic blessing and authority to preach in Germany. Pope Gregory II received him warmly and granted his wishes. "You seem to glow," the Holy Father wrote in his commission, "with the salvation-bringing fire that our Lord came to send upon the earth. Hurry to whatever tribes still linger in the error of unbelief, and institute the rites of the kingdom of God." The pope then gave him a new name: Boniface, "doer of good," the name of an early Roman martyr.

After three years working with the missionary Bishop Willibrord among the Frisians, Boniface returned to Rome—but not without first stopping off in Germany to convert and baptize a few local chieftains. This time the Holy Father consecrated him a bishop and entrusted him with a commission to preach the gospel to the peoples east of the Rhine River "in the shadow of death." For his part, Boniface swore an oath of loyalty to Rome and to maintain "the unity of the one universal Church."

The oath was important because conditions in the German Christian community at that time were chaotic. There were bishops and clergy scattered throughout the kingdom of the Franks—which included the lands we now call France and

Germany—many of whom were untrained and ignored Church law. The personal lives of some made them seem more like wealthy secular nobles than Christian shepherds. The Holy Father knew that these men could cause trouble for devout and energetic missionaries such as Boniface. They would view him as an interloper and an overzealous meddler in the regional affairs of the Church.

For that reason, Boniface's oath declared, in part: "If it comes to my knowledge that priests have turned away from the ancient practices of the holy Fathers, I will have no intercourse or connection with them; rather, I will restrain them if I can. If I cannot, I will at once faithfully make known the whole matter to my apostolic lord."

Thus the missionary's task was twofold: First, he was to preach the gospel to the pagans, so they could come to faith. Second, as Rome's representative he was to help reestablish order in the Frankish Church. Only then could he provide the converts with an environment that would feed spiritual growth rather than scandal.

The Challenges of Mission Ministry

In 723, Boniface returned across the Alps to the Frankish court. There he was formally taken under the protection of the Frankish ruler, Charles Martel. Given the opposition sure to develop to both his missions, this strategy was crucial. Local leaders, religious and secular, would be less likely to oppose him openly if the ruler was his guardian.

Boniface then traveled on to the two regions he had targeted: Hesse and Thuringia. This mission field in central Germany occupied his primary labors for the next fifteen years. There the bishop found a religiously mixed population: the small but faithful Christian flock; the traditional pagans, such as the angry crowd at Geismar; and a curious group in between, who had received baptism yet had fallen back into many of their old beliefs and practices. This last group, Pope Gregory had warned him, were those who had been "led astray by the wiles of the devil and now serve idols under the guise of the Christian religion."

Boniface also had to deal with spiritual charlatans, who confused the people and sought to make themselves spiritual celebrities. A certain Aldebert, a native of Gaul, attracted a great following with claims to work signs and wonders. He told his amazed followers that an angel had given him miracle-working relics, and that he had received a letter sent from heaven, signed by Jesus Christ himself!

Adlebert passed out to the faithful as relics his own nail and hair clippings. He claimed the power to grant absolution without sacramental confession. He invoked in prayer angels with names unrecognized by the Church. Somehow this man even persuaded several naïve Frankish bishops to consecrate him as one of their own. At Boniface's insistence, his teachings, and those of another heretical Frankish bishop named Clement, were finally condemned at a synod in Rome called by the pope in 745.

Undaunted by such an admittedly adverse environment, the missionary set out to preach, build churches, establish monasteries and convents, and confront his lax brother clergy. To fund all the new establishments, Boniface turned to his benefactors in the Frankish court, and to invoke divine help in his efforts, he begged the prayers of a far-flung network of friends and religious colleagues all across Europe. A well-read scholar in a kind of exile on the frontiers of literate culture, Boniface wrote asking for donations of books in order to create libraries for himself and for the monks. Soon friends and even kinfolk from England had come to join him in the missionary task.

Despite such assistance, the bishop's letters from this period reveal just how agonizing was his role. Writing to his former bishop back in England, he sought to confide to his old friend "the troubles of a weary heart." He was surrounded, he wrote sadly, by "false priests and hypocrites" of the Frankish Church who sought to sabotage his work. They failed to share his evangelistic zeal; they were much more interested in joining their wealthy noble friends in lavish hunting expeditions. (Bishop Milo of Trier, in fact, died on one such expedition. He was gored to death by a wild boar in the field.)

Boniface had sworn to the Holy Father not to associate with errant clerics, but his dependence on the Frankish court required him to spend time there, where the disorderly prelates he despised so often clustered like vultures. He had no choice: To evangelize the pagans, he had to reform the clergy. The new Pope Zecharias made him his legate for just that purpose in 741, and the new ruler of the Franks, Charles' son Pepin, also lent his support.

Joining with the secular powers, Boniface resumed the practice of holding church councils among the Frankish bishops—a custom that had been neglected for a generation. Between 742 and 747, no fewer than five councils were held. Boniface presided, and under his leadership new and exacting standards of discipline were established.

By this time the pope had made him an archbishop without see, to strengthen his authority and allow him to consecrate his followers as local bishops. He had wasted no time in training and consecrating men whose character he could trust for new sees in Bavaria and the eastern Frankish Church. Ultimately Boniface was recognized as primate for the bishops of Utrecht (in Frisia), the Rhine, and Germany beyond the Rhine. In 747, he was appointed to the see of Mainz.

Final Missions and Martyrdom

Meanwhile, the aging archbishop wearied of his administrative responsibilities and longed to focus on evangelism once again. "I must soon finish this temporal life, and the course of my days through these infirmities," he wrote an abbot friend. Mission work in areas that were still largely pagan could be dangerous, as he well knew from experience, especially for an old man. But he welcomed the prospect of death for his Lord. So Boniface determined to turn over his episcopal duties to others and return to Frisia, where his mission labors had begun so many years before—a place, according to his first biographer, "he had once departed in body, but never in heart."

In 753, Boniface and his followers set off for the northern coastal regions where the Frisians and Saxons still practiced the old way of life. The archbishop's English ancestors had migrated from this land three centuries before, and his native Saxon tongue was so close to that of the Frisians that he had no problem preaching to the people in a language they could understand. Calling them his kinfolk—"We are of one and the same blood and bone," he insisted—he labored throughout that autumn and the following spring, preaching, building, and baptizing thousands.

On June 5, 754, the vigil of Pentecost, Boniface was camped with his fellow laborers at Dokkum on the coast of Frisia, waiting for a group of newly baptized Catholics to arrive for confirmation. The place lay far to the north, beyond the reach of the Frankish princes who had been his protectors. The party was surprised by a gang of pirates looking for loot.

They rushed into Boniface's tent as he was praying. The elderly missionary—now seventy-five years old, and ill—showed his spunk to the last. When his servants sprang up to fight for him, he told them he had no fear of dying; the day he had long awaited had now come, when he would enter the joy of the Lord.

The pagans attacked with their swords. In an instinctive reflex, the archbishop tried to shield himself with a book; it was later found, slashed twice, with his blood on the pages. Perhaps the old saint had known what was coming; that volume contained a treatise by St. Ambrose: *On the Advantage of Death.*

Of course the book gave way, and the swords found their targets. Boniface and fifty-two companions were martyred that day. The thugs had thought to capture a great booty, but they were sorely disappointed: the baggage was filled with relics and books. Furious, they scattered the items, worthless to them, in the surrounding fields and marshes. A few of the books were later recovered, along with St. Boniface's body, which was taken to rest at last in the great monastery at Fulda.

The saint had fulfilled two of his lifelong goals: to be a missionary, and to be a martyr. In a sense, his long years of weary missionary labor had in fact been a slow martyrdom that was crowned at last on that final day at the seashore. "Let us fight for the Lord in these days of bitterness and affliction," he had once written, feisty as always, to a fellow archbishop. "If this be the will of God, let us die for the holy laws of our fathers, that we may arrive with them at the eternal inheritance."

The Martyrs of Japan

In the following years, St. Boniface's example was imitated by his spiritual children; the Franks themselves and their descendants took their turn as missionaries. Within a couple of centuries, the gospel had penetrated north and east, into Scandinavia and Central Europe, and on into the vast regions we now call Russia. Yet the peoples of the Far East, the far West, and sub-Saharan Africa had to wait much longer to hear the name of Christ.[4]

Not until the mid-sixteenth century did concerted Christian missionary efforts reach Japan. In this distant land, as in many others, the Society of Jesus, founded by St. Ignatius Loyola and six companions in Paris in 1534, played a critical role. The Jesuits, as they were called, took vows to evangelize non-Christians; they displayed a powerful and effective combination of zeal, courage, and willingness to identify closely with the peoples to whom they were sent. As a result, Jesuit missions around the globe brought into the Church many thousands of converts and trained indigenous leaders for the new Christian communities.

St. Francis Xavier, born in Spain and one of the Jesuit order's founding members, brought the Catholic faith to Japan in 1549. The most powerful ruler in Japan, the feudal lord of the city of Yamaguchi, received St. Francis and his little band of priests warmly, authorizing them to preach the Christian faith throughout the empire and permitting Japanese people to embrace it if they wished. The ruler even granted the missionaries a monastery in the city for their residence. Within six months, the Jesuits had won five hundred converts, and even after St. Francis' departure, the mission thrived.

Persecution

Forty years later, Japan's Catholic community had grown to include 200,000 new believers. Nevertheless, the attitude of the rulers eventually changed because of deepening suspicions that the Christian mission would become a stepping stone for Spanish conquest of the nation. Some evidence also suggests that several Buddhist leaders with considerable influence in the government feared the loss of their followers to the new religion and pressed for laws against it. Whatever the reasons for the turnaround in policy, a decree in 1587 ordered all foreign missionaries to leave the country.

Some of the Jesuits obeyed, but others remained and went underground to continue serving their people. The decree was never vigorously enforced, so the missionaries had some freedom to minister, even if under the threat of harassment. In 1596, however, a political incident involving a Spanish vessel led to the arrests of many foreign missionaries—including the Franciscans, who had arrived by this time—and a season of severe persecution began.

For two years the assault on the fledging Japanese church continued; twenty-six native converts were executed at Nagasaki in 1597. Persecution broke out again in 1613, and by 1640 many thousands, both Japanese and foreign, had died. All foreigners were then banished from the nation, and the Christian faith remained outlawed until the latter part of the nineteenth century.

During that anguished period of persecution, many Catholics were subjected to torments that rivaled and even exceeded the horrors of torture in ancient Rome. Some were crucified. Others were frozen to death by exposure in winter.

One group was scalded in boiling water six times a day for thirty-three days, and then at last burned alive slowly at the stake. Those sentenced to death in "the pit" were tightly bound up to the chest and then suspended head down over a pit of human waste. The blood rushed to their heads, but their temples were slashed to allow a slow seepage that prolonged their agony— usually for two or three days.

A more ferocious attack on the Church could hardly be envisioned. Yet, when Catholic missionaries were at last allowed back into the country in 1859, they made a remarkable discovery: Through two centuries of such vehement persecution by the state, thousands of Christians gathered in small communities had secretly kept the faith and passed it down to their descendants— without the aid of priests or formal religious education.

Such spiritual vitality was possible in part through the witness of heroic believers who labored to spread the gospel and paid for their witness with their lives. Though not all their stories will ever be told, perhaps the story of one will suffice to represent them all.

Blessed Michael Nakashima

Michael Nakashima was born in Machiai, Japan, in 1583 to a non-Christian family. Baptized at the age of eleven, he later took a private vow of chastity and lived a holy and penitential life. The "Great Persecution," as it was called, was in progress, and since foreign missionaries were outlawed, he invited a series of fugitive priests to live in his home. Most nights he then went out to gather small groups of Christians, leading them to his house through roundabout paths to elude the government spies. There the believers could receive the precious sacraments in secret.[5]

The risks of taking part in such missionary efforts were great. Nakashima had several close calls. Once he was suspected of harboring fugitives but avoided any formal charges. In 1627, after becoming a Jesuit, he was brought before the district governor. Still no charges could be proven, but he was nonetheless placed under house arrest for a year.

On September 3, 1628, a wood collector came to Nakashima's home to demand firewood to use for an execution—it was the custom in Nagasaki to have the people contribute faggots for burning prisoners alive. This particular prisoner, however, was a missionary, so the young Jesuit refused; he couldn't take part, he said, in the unjust murder of God's minister. The remark was immediately reported to the authorities.

Torture and Martyrdom

Nakashima was arrested and his home was seized. Sent to prison, he was beaten by the guards with clubs in an effort to force his apostasy. Still he stood firm. "Tear me to pieces and rip my soul from my body," he told his tormentors. "But you will never force that detestable word of denial from my mouth."[6]

Next the prison guards subjected Nakashima to the infamous water torture. He was gagged and forced to lie down. Funnels were placed in his nostrils, through which large quantities of water were forced into his body. His torturers next jumped on his abdomen to force the water back out again, and the procedure was repeated multiple times.

The Jesuit's resolve would not be broken. "When the pain became too intense," he later wrote from prison to a friend, "I invoked Our Lady, the Blessed Virgin, and my pain instantly ceased."[7]

By mid-December the enraged officials were ready to try even more severe measures. He was taken to the site of an extinct volcano at Unzen—the Japanese called it "the mouths of hell"—where boiling waters collected in pools in the crater. On Christmas Eve, 1628, a new round of grisly torments began.

First the water torture was repeated. Then the prisoner was made to stand in a shallow pool of the scalding water until the flesh fell from his feet. Next he was placed in a series of pools, each one deeper than the last, until he was standing in boiling water up to his neck.

Once pulled from this last pool, he could no longer walk. In places his bones lay exposed. They threw him on a pile of hay to spend the frigid night in the open. At dawn his persecutors returned, but he was unable to stand up, so they poured the boiling water over his head and body for another two hours.

The only words he spoke as the torturers completed his martyrdom that day were the names of Jesus and Mary. Blessed Nakashima went to be with them, fittingly enough, on Christmas morning.

The Martyrs of North America

While Japanese Jesuits and other Catholics endured such agonies in the East, in the West both Jesuits and Franciscans were taking the gospel to Native American peoples. We've already noted in the introduction the work of the Spanish Franciscans in Georgia. Hundreds of miles to the north, French Jesuits began a mission to the Hurons and other peoples in the Great Lakes region.

These missionaries wrote detailed accounts of their work, providing us with a sometimes startling portrait of life on the French colonial frontier and beyond. Since the Jesuits there often accompanied their native hosts in their travels through the deep forest, they had to adopt the primitive way of life practiced by the natives. Consequently, mission life in America was a life of danger, poverty, toil, and loneliness.[8]

The brothers sometimes spent weeks on foot through the rugged wilderness or braved dangerous rapids in cramped canoes on hunting trips with the natives. On such journeys they typically survived on only a handful of boiled ground corn each day. Travelers slept directly on the rocky ground, out in the open. "During the day," reported one missionary, "the sun burns you; during the night, you run the risk of being a prey to mosquitoes."[9] If the brother should fall ill or injure himself accidentally, the natives had no medicine to help. A seriously incapacitated man might simply be abandoned in the wilderness.

Back at "home" in the Huron camp, things were little better: a miserable hut for shelter, a reed mat or animal skin for a bed. In the summer, fleas, sand flies, and other vermin tormented them without mercy. In the winter, the missionaries couldn't decide which was worse: braving the bitter cold or breathing the thick smoke that filled the huts and burned their eyes.

As if the rigors of primitive surroundings were not difficult enough, the Jesuits also had to deal with certain cultural habits of the native people that made evangelism all the more a challenge. In 1611, one priest reported to his superior that many of his new acquaintances were "savage, haunting the forests, ignorant, lawless and rude." Often he found them "extremely lazy, gluttonous, profane, treacherous, cruel in their vengeance, and given over to all kinds of lewdness, both men and women."[10] The men shared multiple wives, abused them physically, and treated them like slaves.

Nevertheless, the missionaries recognized that these were people made in God's own image, people for whom Christ had died. In his instructions for evangelism, the pioneer missionary French Jesuit St. Jean de Brébeuf reminded the brothers: "You must have sincere affection for the savages, seeing them as ransomed by the blood of the Son of God, and as our brethren, with whom we will pass the rest of our lives." Personally responsible for some seven thousand conversions among the Hurons, Brébeuf ultimately gave his life for the mission when he was captured, cruelly tortured, and murdered by their bitter enemies, the Iroquois.

St. Isaac Jogues

One of the most famous of the North American martyrs was the French missionary St. Isaac Jogues. Born in Orleans in 1607, he entered the Jesuit novitiate at the age of seventeen, studied theology and philosophy in Paris, and was ordained in 1636. No doubt he first heard of his brother missionaries in New France through one of his teachers, who had a brother and two nephews serving there. In addition, in 1629 he had met Brébeuf, who was visiting France during the British occupation of Quebec.

Six months after his ordination, Jogues himself left for America. He arrived in Quebec, and in the summer of 1636 he set out for his first mission to Huronia—nine hundred miles away—by canoe and on foot. There he met up with Brébeuf and set about learning the Huron language and instructing the people in the faith.

The first clear threats of death came when smallpox swept the village, and the Black Robes, as the Jesuits were called, were blamed for the epidemic. The local shaman found all remedies useless, so the Hurons threatened to kill all the foreigners. Brébeuf conciliated them, however, and circumstances improved.

Jogues ministered with success in the village of Sainte-Marie; among his first group of 120 adult converts was the tribe's greatest war chief. Yet the missionary longed to see the entire tribe converted, and one day in prayer he told God he would undergo any hardship to see the faith firmly planted among them. He believed he heard God's answer clearly: "Let it be done to you as you have asked. Be comforted! Have a strong heart!"

First Encounter With the Iroquois

In 1642 Jogues journeyed with a group of Hurons to a distant settlement to obtain supplies, and then on to Quebec to ask for additional missionaries. René Goupil, a surgeon and lay assistant to the Jesuits, returned with him. On the way home, the party was attacked and overwhelmed by Mohawk warriors. The Mohawks were members of the confederation of Five Nations of the Iroquois, old enemies of the Hurons, who were then at war with the French as well.

These particular natives believed that the more cruel they were to their enemies, the more fortunate they would be in battle. Their victims soon discovered just how cruel such men could be. When Jogues tried to tend to a wounded Frenchman, the Mohawks beat him, bit out his fingernails, and chewed off his forefingers. Goupil suffered similar atrocities.

The prisoners were then taken to a distant Mohawk village. On the way, the natives met some of their own people and stopped to display their captives and to torture them. Jogues and his companions were forced to strip and run up a rocky hill between two rows of warriors, one hundred on each side, who beat them mercilessly with sticks and thorns as they passed.

Taking the prisoners on to their destination, the Mohawks forced them through the gauntlet a second time. This time Jogues was made to run last so he could receive his tormentors' focused attention. Halfway through the gauntlet he fell, and the mob rushed upon him with their clubs. After nearly killing him, they bound his bleeding body to a platform they had built and began to jeer and taunt him. The blows began once again over his entire body.

Next the savage torturers burned one of his fingers, crushed another with their teeth, and twisted and squeezed the others they had already injured. They stabbed him and scratched his wounds with their fingernails, then laid burning torches to his arms and thighs. The other prisoners received similar abuse.

One woman of the village cut off the priest's left thumb with a jagged shell. Then Jogues and Goupil were tied to the ground so that children could drop red-hot coals on their naked bodies. Such torments continued for a full three days.

Finally the two men were given as personal slaves to the chief who captured them. Only a few weeks later Goupil was tomahawked to death for making the sign of the cross over a young girl. The local shaman had declared that the gesture was sorcery.

Throughout the months of his captivity, Jogues was the object of the villagers' perpetual scorn, and they compelled him to perform the most degrading kinds of labor. Nevertheless, he was able to minister to the Christian Huron captives of the village. He baptized children he found dying. Occasionally he was even able to catch a few moments alone in the forest to kneel, pray, and recite Scripture before a cross he had carved into the bark of a great tree.

After a year of slavery, Jogues went with his masters to visit a Dutch trading settlement. The Dutch bravely helped him escape, hid him on one of their ships, and paid the Mohawks a ransom for him. Then they took him to their colony at New Amsterdam—now New York City—where he finally obtained passage back to France. He arrived there on Christmas morning, 1643.

His Jesuit brothers in France received him with great honor as a hero, and he had ample reason for joy. Yet, to the priest's great sorrow, he was no longer able to celebrate Mass, because of his mutilated hands—he couldn't hold the Host correctly. The brothers asked the Pope for a dispensation, however, and he granted it enthusiastically. "It would be shameful," he said, "if a martyr of Christ were not allowed to drink the blood of Christ."[11]

Back to America

After a few months of recuperation in France, Jogues began to think the unthinkable. Despite all he'd suffered, he would go back to the mission field—not just to the Hurons, but to the Mohawks.

After one last visit to his mother in Orleans, he sailed back to New France in the spring of 1644. Terms of peace had at last been hammered out between the French and the Iroquois confederation, so Jogues' superior granted him permission to minister to the Mohawks if the opportunity arose. In September the Hurons were invited by the Mohawks to send an embassy to discuss details of the treaty, and Jogues joined them, accompanied by the French lay missionary assistant John de La Lande.

In a letter written to friends in France just before he left, the Jesuit noted: "I shall go, but I shall not return. I will be happy if Our Lord will be pleased to complete the sacrifice there where he began it, and make the little blood I have shed in that land the earnest of what I would give from every vein of my body and my heart."

A few days after they began their journey, word came that the Mohawks were again on the warpath. All but one of the Hurons turned back in fear, yet Jogues, La Lande, and the lone native pressed on. The residents of the village where Jogues had been held captive were convinced that a black chest of religious items he'd left with them had magically caused a famine and epidemic, so when a Mohawk scouting party looking for Frenchmen to kill came upon the little band on October 17, they shrieked excitedly.

Martyrdom

The three men were seized, stripped, and run through the gauntlet. Then they were dragged into the village, where Jogues had strips of flesh cut from his neck and arms. The next day, October 18, 1644, one of his captors invited him to feast at the chief's lodge.

The priest knew it was a trap, but he couldn't refuse the invitation without causing offense. As soon as he entered the chief's lodge, a Mohawk warrior struck him dead with a tomahawk. La Lande's murder followed the next day. The bodies of the two missionaries were beheaded, their heads were exposed on the palisades around the village, and their bodies were thrown into the Mohawk River.

Three years later Fr. Jean de Brébeuf, who had been Jogues' hero, followed him in martyrdom. On March 16, 1649, the Iroquois captured him and several companions, then employed the same tortures Jogues had suffered—the gauntlet, fire, flaying, mutilation of hands. But to these brutalities still more outrageous horrors were added.

A half dozen iron hatchets were heated until they glowed red, then strung as a "necklace" and hung on the victims' shoulders. One of Brébeuf's companions had his hands cut off and his eyes gouged out. Burning coals were then put in his empty eye sockets.

Brébeuf's torso was wrapped in resinous bark and set aflame. Instead of crying out, the priest only exhorted the other Christians to remain steadfast in their suffering. His captors silenced him by cutting off his nose, ripping off his lips, and forcing a hot iron down his throat.

As a mockery of baptism, kettles of scalding water were poured over the missionary's head. Then he was scalped by one torturer while another chopped off his feet. His jaw was cut off from his face with a hatchet. As a final indignity, some of the warriors sliced strips of his seared flesh and ate them. Others cut open his chest, tore out his heart, and devoured it.

In the days to follow the Iroquois continued to attack and plunder the Huron villages, and there were other martyrs, both native and foreign. Yet throughout the Mohawk Valley, those who died were venerated for having possessed to a heroic degree the virtue that the native peoples most admired: bravery. In time, new missionaries found a welcome, even among the Iroquois, where a new harvest of souls proved that the sufferings of the faithful had not been in vain.

The Martyrs of Uganda

Nineteenth-century Catholic missions to black Africa resulted in numerous clashes between the mores of traditional cultures and the moral demands of the new faith. Uganda's first Catholic martyrs were executed because they challenged the attempts of a local chieftain to force himself sexually on Christian youth. These brave believers distinguished themselves among the Church's missionary martyrs, in that several were children and teenagers, and nearly all were laypeople, most of whom were taking an active role in the task of evangelism.

King Mwanga of Buganda (part of what is now Uganda) was a tyrant who expected utter submission to his every whim. The troubles began when he learned that his head steward, a Catholic lay catechist named Joseph Mukasa, was intervening to keep several Christian pages out of his bed.[12]

Mukasa had already earned the king's ire by openly challenging a royal order to massacre seven Anglican missionaries. Yet he placed himself in even greater danger by protecting the pages. Whenever the king would send for a boy in order to abuse him, Mukasa would hide him in his own home or send him away out of the king's reach. Finally, Mwanga found an excuse to get rid of the popular steward: When Mukasa gave him an opium pill during an illness, the king claimed that he'd tried to poison him.

Mwanga ordered the steward to be burned alive. As Joseph walked to his death, he told the guards there was no need to tie him up. "Why should you bind me?" he asked. "From whom should I escape? From God?"

The executioner liked Mukasa and was reluctant to carry out the sentence. At last he decided to minimize the young catechist's agony by beheading him instead. Before he died, Mukasa gave him a message for the king: "Tell Mwanga I forgive him for putting me to death without a reason, but let him repent. Otherwise, I will accuse him in God's court."

At age twenty-six, St. Joseph was the first Catholic martyr of Uganda, dying in 1885. He was soon followed by others who resisted the perversion of the king. Though Mwanga announced his intentions to "kill all those who pray," several Catholic catechumens remained at the court and prepared themselves for martyrdom. Among them was St. Charles Lwanga, who took Mukasa's place as head steward.

Lwanga bravely continued his predecessor's policy of protecting the pages from the king's lust by hiding them. Royal retribution was delayed, however, when a series of events convinced the superstitious ruler that his killing of Mukasa had brought a curse on him. The martyr's final message had haunted him, and twelve days after Mukasa died there had been a meteor shower. That was followed by a number of fires in the royal compound and a lightning strike on one of the huts. To Mwanga, these were all ill omens.

Rage overcame his fear, however, when he returned from an unsuccessful hunt one day to find all the Christian pages missing. One of them returned and confessed to having been receiving instruction from a sixteen-year-old catechist named

Denis Ssebuggwawo. The furious king summoned the teenager, speared him with a lance, and had the page executed.

The Christian pages were urged to hide, but they remained, and Mwanga shut the gates of the royal compound. He called for his chiefs and executioners. Meanwhile, Lwanga led the young pages all night in prayer. Some who hadn't yet received baptism received the sacrament, among them the youngest page, a small boy named Kizito. Then Lwanga urged them all to confess the faith bravely.

When the king summoned the prisoners to appear before his assembly, he issued an order for "all those who pray" to stand in a certain place. Little Kizito took Lwanga's hand and they walked over to the spot. They were followed by the other Christian pages, who were then joined by several others: Bruno Serunkuma; one of the royal bodyguards; a sixteen-year-old pagan page who had been secretly receiving Christian instruction; and the adopted son of the chief executioner.

The executioner ordered his young son to hide, but the boy didn't move. Another executioner admonished him to obey his father. The child replied respectfully: "My Father whom I must obey is in heaven."

The prisoners then began a death march to their place of execution, which took them through several villages over the course of sixteen miles. Some were killed along the way. Matthias Mulumba, the oldest, had his limbs hacked off, and as he watched, pieces of his flesh were burned. To prolong his torment, his major arteries and veins were tied off, then he was left alone in the sun to die several days later.

One of the martyrs was speared and thrown onto an anthill; another was wounded and tied to a tree, where the wild dogs would come to finish him off. At their destination the rest of the

Christians were imprisoned for several days. In the end, they were wrapped in reed mats or tied to stakes and burned alive.

Nevertheless, the words of St. Bruno to his brother on the way to his death proved to be prophetic: "A fountain fed from many springs will never dry up. When we are gone, others will rise in our place." The executioner, who had only snickered when Lwanga had invited him to convert, eventually embraced the faith. Today, a third of the population of Uganda belongs to the Catholic Church.

SIX

"MY GREATEST ENEMIES, MY BEST FRIENDS"
Martyrs Killed by Other Christians

Jesus answered ... "Indeed, the hour is coming when whoever kills you will think he is offering service to God."

JOHN 14:23; 16:2

A martyrdom borne for the sake of preventing a division of the Church would not have been less glorious than one endured for refusing to worship idols. No—in my opinion, in fact, the former would have been a nobler thing than the latter. For in the one case, a person gives such a testimony simply for his own individual soul; while in the other case, he is a witness for the whole Church.

St. Dionysius the Great, *Epistles*, 2

When the early Christians went bravely to their deaths at the hands of the pagans, could they ever have even dreamed that one day their spiritual descendants would murder one another for their faith?

To write of martyrs killed by their Christian brothers and sisters raises a number of thorny and sensitive issues. However, such martyrs must not be forgotten; they too gave their lives for Christ. In their stories, we're reminded just how twisted even the best of intentions can become, how thoroughly we human beings can deceive ourselves into thinking that by acting on our passions we're somehow performing a "service to God" (Jn 16:2).

This book limits itself to the stories of martyrs of the Catholic Church. When we speak only of Catholic martyrs in this particular context, however, we run several risks. First, we may leave the impression that the tables were never turned—that non-Catholics have never been killed by Catholics for their faith. Tragically, that is not at all the case, as was confirmed by the recent Jubilee year apology of Pope John Paul II for the past sins of Catholics. In fact, some Catholic martyrs were actually killed by other Catholics, as the story of St. Thomas à Becket illustrates.

Second, we may seem to be suggesting that hatred for Catholics is somehow an inherent part of belief and practice among Christians who are separated from the Church of Rome. Nothing, of course, could be further from the truth. The daring rescue of St. Isaac Jogues by Dutch Calvinists in colonial America, as was noted in the last chapter, should serve as a firm reminder that Christ's own love can shine across denominational barriers despite quite serious differences in theology.

Finally, we should note here what Pope John Paul II repeatedly pointed out in the Jubilee year: Since nearly every historic Christian community has contributed its share of men and women who died for their faith, the martyrs have the power to advance the cause of Christian unity as they all point toward their common Lord, Jesus Christ. Speaking at the ecumenical commemoration of the martyrs in the Coliseum during the Jubilee year, the Holy Father observed: "The precious heritage that these courageous witnesses have passed down to us is a patrimony shared by all the Churches and ecclesial communities. It is a heritage that speaks more powerfully than all the causes of division. The ecumenism of the martyrs and of the witnesses to the faith is the most convincing of all; to the Christians of the twentieth century it shows the path to unity."[1]

Though the scope of this book is necessarily limited, then, we should read these accounts of Catholics killed by other Christians as one chapter in a larger story, not just of tragic fratricidal strife, but also of heroic ecumenical witness.

St. Flavian of Constantinople

If early Christians would have been stunned to know that later believers sometimes killed one another for their faith, perhaps most Christians today would be scandalized to hear the story of St. Flavian. This fifth-century patriarch (that is, an archbishop of the East) died from a violent assault by a fellow archbishop and an abbot—while attending a Church council! Flavian suffered martyrdom because of his insistence that a particular ancient heresy contradicted the truths of the Catholic faith.[2]

He became Patriarch of Constantinople—in the ancient Church an honor second in esteem only to the pope—in A.D. 447. By that time the great persecutions were over; the Roman imperial government had largely turned from paganism and embraced the Christian faith. Nevertheless, especially in the East, where the empire had its new capital at Constantinople (now Istanbul, Turkey), imperial politics and church politics had become dangerously entwined.

The emperors at that time decided who would lead the church in the capital city. Yet even though Flavian was the choice of Emperor Theodosius II, the new patriarch immediately encountered friction with his court. A court eunuch named Chrysaphius, a chamberlain and favorite of the emperor, persuaded the ruler to require from Flavian a gift to show his "gratitude" for the appointment.

In those days, bishops customarily bestowed a gift of blessed bread as a token of benediction and a sign of communion. Flavian honored that tradition. Chrysaphius indignantly informed the prelate that the emperor had something else in mind: gold.

Such a gift, replied Flavian, would constitute simony—the sin of buying ecclesiastical office. The treasures and funds of the Church were to be used only for God's glory and to care for the poor. The eunuch was outraged and began to plot revenge.

Combat With Heresy

The next year, Chrysaphius' fury against the patriarch intensified when Flavian publicly condemned the theological errors of the eunuch's godfather, Eutyches, abbot of a large monastery near the capital city. Eutyches denied that Christ's human nature was of the same substance as our own. He also insisted that once God the Son had taken on human nature in the Incarnation, there were no longer two distinct natures, one divine and one human, within the one person of Christ. (This last heresy is known as *monophysitism*, from the Greek term for "one nature.")

Flavian, and the Catholic Church as a whole, rightly rejected these doctrines as incompatible with divine Revelation. If the human nature God joined to himself in Christ had been unlike ours, then Christ would have been in some sense alien to us; our nature would not have been redeemed by him. And if that joining of two natures in Christ had resulted in a single nature, then Christ's humanity would have been swallowed up and lost in his divinity. On both counts Eutyches had misunderstood the full reality of the Incarnation: In Christ, God joined to himself a human nature just like ours, and that human nature was never lost.

In 448 Flavian presided over a local Church council at which Eutyches appeared with two officers of the court and a troop of imperial guards. Expecting that this unmistakable show of the court's favor would intimidate the thirty-two bishops and twenty-three abbots assembled, Eutyches insisted that his teachings were correct. When the fathers attempted to show him his error, he declared arrogantly that he had not come to debate them on the disputed points. Since he refused to change his position, the council had no choice but to condemn his teachings and depose him from his position as abbot.

The "Den of Robbers"

Eutyches appealed the decision to Pope St. Leo, but when the Holy Father read a transcript of the council proceedings sent by Flavian, he was appalled at the abbot's false doctrines and added his own condemnation to them. Nevertheless, Eutyches was busy at the imperial court, using his influence through Chrysaphius to persuade Theodosius to intervene. The emperor called a new council to meet at the city of Ephesus in 669.

The pope declined to attend this meeting, but he sent legates and a doctrinal statement, the famous "Tome of Leo," addressed to Flavian and outlining the orthodox position of the Church. Eutyches and his friends at court—including the empress Eudoxia—made certain, however, that the new council was largely composed of Church leaders who were jealous of the power and honor held by the patriarch of Constantinople. They refused even to allow the letter from the pope to be read.

A large contingent of imperial officers and soldiers at the meetings left no doubt that the emperor wanted a reversal of the abbot's condemnation. Dioscorus, the archbishop of Antioch—for many years, a rival see of Constantinople—had been assigned by the emperor to preside over the meeting.

When he read aloud a judgment overturning the previous council's pronouncements and deposing Flavian instead, the pope's legates protested strenuously, but to no avail.

Several bishops prostrated themselves before Dioscorus, begging him to cease the proceedings. At that point he called aloud for the imperial commissioners to open the doors of the church where they were meeting. Immediately the Roman proconsul entered with a band of soldiers, followed by a mob armed with chains, clubs, and swords.

Under this violent coercion nearly all the bishops present signed the judgment. The pope's legates refused, however, and continued their vocal protest. One was eventually imprisoned, while the other escaped with great difficulty and returned to Rome.

When Flavian heard the sentence read by Dioscorus, he appealed to the pope and gave his acts of appeal in writing to the papal legates. Dioscorus flew into a rage at the action, and along with an abbot and others in his faction, he threw the archbishop to the ground and attacked him with kicks and blows. Carried away to exile in another city, Flavian died a few days later from the injuries received in the assault.

Dioscorus next had the audacity to excommunicate the Holy Father. Justice, however, was not long in coming. St. Leo condemned the violent proceedings at Ephesus as a false council; the *latrocinium*, he called it—the "den of robbers." Chrysaphius soon disgraced himself at court and was put to death; the empress Eudoxia was forced to retire from the court and withdraw in humiliation to Palestine. The next year the emperor Theodosius fell off his horse and died.

Meanwhile, Flavian's relics were brought to Constantinople with great honor, to be interred with those of his predecessors. The papal legate to Ephesus later became pope himself. The next ecumenical council, which met at Chalcedon in 451, declared Flavian a saint and martyr, condemned and deposed Dioscorus, and defined Catholic orthodoxy on the issues involving Christ's two natures, approving Pope St. Leo's tome as a clear statement of the faith of the Church. In the end, the great truth about Christ to which Flavian had borne witness came to prevail.

St. Thomas à Becket
The Unlikely Martyr

Ancient Constantinople wasn't the only place in Church history where the volatile mix of secular and ecclesiastical politics led to martyrdoms. Affairs at the royal court in medieval England led to the murder of another archbishop—Thomas à Becket of Canterbury—whose heroism made him the nation's most illustrious saint.[3]

Born in London in 1118 to wealthy Norman parents, Becket studied first at several English schools, then at Paris, and finally at the university in Bologna, the chief European center for the study of law. He was ordained a deacon and eventually appointed archdeacon of Canterbury in 1154. The next year, King Henry II made him chancellor, for he was an exceptionally competent statesman, and the two men were close friends.

In many ways, Becket was the most unlikely of martyrs. He was immensely wealthy and given to the leisurely occupations of his class: feasting, hunting, and hawking. As chancellor, his policies typically reflected the king's wishes, even when such policies weren't in the best interests of the Church; one of the English bishops went so far as to call him a "persecutor of the Church." He sometimes led hundreds of soldiers into battle for the king, showing no mercy to the enemies of England.

Becket enjoyed the privileges of his office, especially the opportunity it afforded him to display great pomp. On one visit to the king of France in 1158, for example, he crossed the English Channel with six frigates and a retinue of two thousand. As his party made its way through French cities on the way to Paris, he was preceded by 250 musicians, surrounded by a large pack of pet greyhounds, and followed by eight carriages, each pulled by six horses. Next came wagons carrying his bedroom, kitchen, chapel, and silver. Last in the parade were hundreds of horsemen on proud chargers, all arrayed in silver and gold.

Becket was only a deacon, but in 1162, at the instigation of the king, he was chosen to become archbishop of Canterbury—an office whose occupant held first place, both in honor and in influence, in the Catholic Church in England. The reluctant candidate was ordained a priest on June 1 and consecrated a bishop two days later.

Though the king was, of course, a member of the Catholic Church himself, he shared the priority held by most rulers: The maintenance and extension of his own power trumped all other concerns. Henry was convinced that his right-hand man and old hunting buddy would make the perfect tool for pressing the power of the state more deeply into the affairs of the Church. Think of it—the most powerful secular official in the nation after the king would be at the same time the most powerful church official in the realm! And both offices would be under the tight control of the king himself.

Henry, however, was terribly mistaken. Even Becket saw right away the untenable position in which he would be placed. When first informed of the king's intentions, he said glumly: "If I should by chance be promoted, I would either lose the favor of my lord the king ... or neglect the service of the Lord God."

Conflict With the King

We may have in Becket's case clear historical evidence for the sacramental grace bestowed in Holy Orders. Once the hands were imposed on Thomas' head to make him a priest, his entire way of life changed. The man of wealth and leisure began to practice austere penances to purify himself. According to his own later account, he was transformed from "a follower of hounds to a shepherd of souls."

Within weeks, Thomas was spending hours every morning in prayer. He secretly wore a penitential hair shirt beneath his splendid robe. He lavished his wealth on the poor. Every morning before dawn, after matins had been sung, he invited thirteen people from among the poor to feast at the episcopal residence. He himself washed their feet and waited on them at the table. When they were done, he sent them away with a gift of four silver coins each, asking them to pray for him.

When he sat down to his own table, the archbishop ate sparingly. The minstrels and actors once employed for mealtime entertainment were now replaced with readings from Scripture and other religious books.

Though Henry must have found all this perplexing, his confusion turned to annoyance when Becket resigned the chancellorship. That secular office, the new archbishop insisted, was incompatible with his responsibilities over Christ's flock. As conflicts arose between Church and state in the days following, Henry found, to his great consternation, that Becket showed himself loyal first to spiritual priorities and to the Holy Father in Rome.

Only a year after the new archbishop was consecrated, a crucial dispute arose over the respective jurisdictions of secular and ecclesiastical courts. This was an old and troublesome debate in England that had provoked dissension for generations.

Henry required the English bishops to affirm, among other proposed laws, that clerics found guilty of crimes in ecclesiastical courts should also be turned over to the civil courts.

Becket opposed the idea: first, because he agreed with the standing arrangement that clergymen were best judged by bishops, rather than by laymen; and second, because the process involved two trials and two punishments for the same offense. As canon law declared, "God does not judge the same case twice."

The issue was made even more serious by the Church's law forbidding ecclesiastical courts to shed blood. Thus a crime punishable in civil courts by what were often savage penalties— the gouging out of eyes, for example, or the amputation of hands—would receive from the Church a stiff prison term or fine instead.

The pope opposed Henry's new legislation; Becket stood with Rome. He sensed that establishing such a precedent of capitulation to the state would only lead to more drastic demands. Henry's angry words to the bishops who had assembled with Thomas to present their position suggested that the king ultimately had more than court jurisdictions in mind. "I demand," he shouted, "absolute and express agreement with my customs!"

Still Becket refused. Henry stormed out of the council hall, but the next day he summoned Becket and attempted once more, this time in private, to make him submit. When the king reminded him of his sworn loyalty to the throne, Becket's reply was firm:

"You are indeed my lord, but God is my Lord and yours. It would be useful neither to you nor to me if I were to neglect his will in order to obey yours. For on his fearful judgment day, you and I will both be judged as servants of one Lord."

After Becket's final refusal, a series of reprisals were launched against him, including trumped up charges that he had mismanaged funds while chancellor. Henry summoned Becket to appear before a council of bishops and barons at Northampton for a trial. When it became clear that the king was seeking revenge more than justice, however, Thomas fled the country, taking refuge in France with King Louis VII.

Becket remained four years in exile. As the rift between Henry and Rome widened, the pope excommunicated two disobedient English bishops and threatened to put England under the interdict—that is, a papal decree suspending nearly all administration of the sacraments and celebration of solemn services, throughout the entire country. In 1169, however, Henry finally worked out a reconciliation with Rome, and the next year Becket returned to England.

The king assumed at this point that the archbishop had been chastened and would give him no further trouble. Again, Henry was terribly mistaken. Becket continued to defend the prerogatives of the Church against the pretensions of the secular state.

Martyrdom

One day in the royal court, while lamenting his problems with Becket, in a fit of anger Henry cried out, "What disloyal cowards I have in my court, that no one will free me of this wretched priest!" Four barons who were present heard in those words a summons to execute the archbishop and be done with him.

Secretly the four knights agreed to commit the deed, then slipped away from the court. Meanwhile, other barons began to speak more openly of treating Becket to a rope and gibbet. Henry offered no rebuke to such threats.

Becket received word in Canterbury that some of the king's

men were coming for him. When a member of his household brought news confirming the danger, he replied simply: "I think I know for certain that I will be slain. But they will find me ready to suffer pain and death for God's name."

On December 8, 1170, the barons arrived at the archbishop's palace to threaten him. "If all the swords in England hung over my head," he thundered in reply, "you could not turn me from God's justice and my obedience to the pope! You will find me ready to meet you eye to eye in the Lord's battle."

The men left to arm themselves, still breathing threats, but when it was time for vespers, Becket went to the cathedral. Monks of the surrounding cloister barred the church doors; Becket ordered them to be opened. "Christ's Church is not a fortress," he insisted. No one moved, so he slid back the bolts himself.

In the gathering dark, Thomas' companions could hear his enemies coming. They found hiding places in the cavernous church. He could have joined them, but instead, he took his place between the chapel of Our Lady and the chapel of St. Benedict, then turned to face his pursuers. The four barons, now armed with swords, met him there.

An attacker took hold of his cloak; for a moment, the old Thomas seemed to be speaking when he shouted, "Take your hands off me, you pimp!" A struggle ensued. Only one of Becket's friends came to his aid. When one of the swords grazed his head, the archbishop ceased all resistance, bowed his head, and prayed.

One of his enemies brought down his sword, but his sole defender deflected it with his arm, so that the resulting blow to Becket's head was bloody, but not fatal. Another sword stroke to his head left him still standing and praying. Under a third blow, he fell to his hands and knees, murmuring his last words:

"For the name of Jesus and the defense of the Church, I embrace death."

The final deathblow was so forceful that the sword's blade shattered in two on the stone floor, and the crown of the martyr's head was cut away. As a final insult, one of the men standing nearby placed his foot on the neck of the corpse, thrust his sword into the head wound, and scattered brains and blood across the floor. "Let's go, knights," he said. "This fellow won't rise again."

He was wrong. That night, one of the monks saw Thomas in a vision, dressed in his vestments and "beautiful to look upon." The monk asked him, "Aren't you dead, my lord?"

"I was dead," the martyr replied, "but I have risen again."

Veneration of the Saint

Despite an unusual winter thunderstorm that began that night after the murderers left, the townsfolk flooded to the cathedral to view the martyr. The common people had loved him dearly, and they cut pieces from their clothing, dipped it in his blood, and despite their sorrow thanked God for a new saint. Within a few days, reports began to come in of miracles attributed to his intercession. More than five hundred were recorded in the next few years, all over Europe.

News of the outrage spread quickly across the Channel and throughout the Continent. Before long, pilgrims were coming to Becket's tomb by the thousands, and eventually by the tens of thousands. From Palestine to Iceland, the name of Thomas was invoked, and in 1173 the Holy Father gave official recognition to his sainthood.

When Henry heard what had happened, he wailed and fell into a stupor; those around him feared for his sanity. He confessed publicly to having been the unwitting cause of the crime and agreed to whatever penances the Church would impose on him. Among the conditions required by Rome was his renunciation of the legislation that had first caused his rift with Becket.

In 1174, Henry himself came to Canterbury to seek peace with his old friend. Armed rebellion was rending the nation; the king was desperate for help to restore peace. Henry fasted, dressed in a hair shirt and the woolen tunic of the pilgrim, and walked barefoot in the rain to the cathedral. There he knelt to weep and pray at the martyr's tomb, then submitted to flagellation by the bishops, the abbot, and eighty monks.

The next day, word arrived that a major leader of the rebellion had just been captured—immediately after Henry had completed his penance—and the back of the resistance had been broken. "God be thanked for it!" the king shouted, "and St. Thomas the martyr and all the saints of God!"

From the throne on down, England now acknowledged its indebtedness to Becket, the unlikely martyr.

St. Thomas More

Becket's shrine remained one of Christendom's most popular pilgrim sites for nearly four hundred years. (It was, in fact, the destination of the pilgrims featured in Geoffrey Chaucer's celebrated fourteenth-century classic, *Canterbury Tales*.) But in 1538, yet another King Henry of England—this one, the Eighth—declared himself the saint's enemy. Having put to death his own chancellor named Thomas for refusing to betray the Church (history does sometimes repeat itself), Henry demolished Becket's shrine, consigned his bones to an unmarked grave, and stole the treasures of gold, silver, and jewels with which countless devotees had endowed the spot.

Images of the saint found anywhere in the churches of England were ordered to be destroyed. His name was to be erased from the liturgy and the prayer books. Becket was a symbol reminding the world that the Catholic Church was not a vassal of the English crown, and for that the latter-day Henry hated him.

Of course, all such violence did infinitely more harm to England than to St. Thomas, who was safely out of the king's reach. Yet Henry wasn't content just to assault the memory of the dead. He vented his wrath on living targets as well. Other Catholic martyrs in England and all across Europe were soon joining the ranks of the blessed. The Protestant Reformation had ruptured the unity of the Church; Christians were fighting Christians; and Catholics were being called to witness with their blood to the ancient faith of their fathers.

Politics and Passions

St. Thomas More had been among the first to die, in 1535. A skilled lawyer and statesman, brilliant Renaissance scholar, successful businessman, and beloved family man, More had carved for himself—as Becket had done—a place of trust and friendship at the side of the king. Henry VIII made him his chancellor and confidant.[4]

Ironically, only a few years after the Reformation first erupted in 1517 with Martin Luther's actions in Germany, King Henry had responded by publishing a learned treatise in defense of the Catholic Church. The work had earned him from Pope Leo X the title "Defender of the Faith." Luther had answered with characteristic vehemence, publishing an attack on Henry, and it was Thomas More who had come to the king's defense with an equally spirited reply to Luther.

In the intervening years, however, politics and personal passions had come to cloud Henry's judgment. His Spanish wife had borne him no sons, and he was growing concerned that he might not leave a male heir. At the same time, he was infatuated with Anne Boleyn, his determined mistress, who wanted to be his queen instead. So Henry asked the pope to grant him a divorce from his wife. Rome said no.

Since Henry wouldn't take no for an answer, he settled on a different strategy—one with perilous implications for the English Church. The king pressed Parliament to pass legislation repudiating the authority of the pope and making himself the "head" of the Church in England. Repressive measures against clergymen who opposed the measures pressured many of them, including bishops, to join him in the national schism.

Meanwhile, the king had his new "Anglican" archbishop of Canterbury declare the royal marriage null and recognize a new marriage to his mistress. Anne Boleyn was crowned queen (though only for three years—the king ultimately divorced her in turn to marry another mistress, and had Boleyn executed). The pope, for his part, excommunicated Henry and annulled his divorce and remarriage.

Not long after, Henry ordered the Catholic religious orders in England to be dissolved. Their wealth he confiscated for his own coffers or distributed to his political cronies. Other measures taken by the king, Parliament, and the schismatic bishops in the days to come would make it clear that the new Anglican ecclesiastical structure had done more than break communion with Rome. It had begun a theological and liturgical revolution that placed it squarely within the emerging Protestant camp.

Within a generation, the remaining English Catholics—and there were many thousands of them—would be forced to live their faith secretly. Many would be hunted down, fined, imprisoned, tortured, and even executed for the faith that Henry had once so publicly defended.

Imprisonment

Thomas More, a firm and faithful lay son of the Catholic Church, could not in good conscience go along with Henry's schemes. He opposed the royal divorce and in 1532 tendered his resignation as chancellor of the realm—leaving him and his family with almost no income. The Duke of Norfolk warned him that he was in danger; to insult the king's dignity, he suggested, was death.

"Is that all, my lord?" replied More. "Well, then, there is only one difference between your grace and me: I will die today, and you, tomorrow."

In 1534, the Act of Succession was passed by Parliament, requiring that anyone of whom it was demanded must take an oath recognizing Anne Boleyn's children as legitimate heirs to the throne. It also repudiated "any foreign authority, prince or potentate." More refused the oath; it implicitly affirmed the validity of the king's second marriage and denied papal authority. A few weeks later he was arrested and imprisoned in the Tower of London.

More turned his fifteen-month imprisonment into an occasion for prayer, penance, and the production of the most inspired works of a long literary career. Among these devotional classics were his *Dialogue of Comfort Against Tribulation,* his *Treatise on the Passion of Christ,* and his meditation *On the Sadness of Christ,* along with several profound and deeply moving prayers. Though he struggled mightily with doubts and fears during this time, his characteristic gaiety remained intact whenever he wrote letters to friends and family or received visits from them.

In July of 1535 More was convicted of high treason on the grounds of having opposed the Act of Supremacy that made Henry "Supreme Head" of the Church in England. He was sentenced to death. All his adult life More had written that meditation on death was a good spiritual medicine, because it freed the soul from undue attachments to things that quickly pass away. He had taken his own medicine; he had let go of this world; he was ready now for the executioner.

The Merry Saint

More's indomitable sense of humor had long reflected his detachment: After all, to be *in* the world but not *of* the world is, among other things, to laugh at the world. Yet even the friends who knew him best may well have been startled by the lightness of heart he displayed on his way to die.

Weary and with his hands tied behind his back, he feared that he might stumble on the rickety steps of the scaffold as he went to be beheaded. Turning to the lieutenant beside him, he quipped, "I pray you, see me safely up, and for my coming down let me shift for myself."

Next, More embraced his executioner, gave him a piece of gold, and told him: "Courage, my good man; don't be afraid. But take care—I've got a short neck, and you don't want to embarrass yourself!"

Even when he laid his head on the block, the banter continued. More asked the executioner to wait while he moved aside his beard. After all, he quipped, his *beard* had never committed treason![5]

Thus did the merry saint depart this life. His oppressors didn't appreciate his humor, but it didn't matter: He had forgiven them anyway, long before. In the dark silence of the tower, he'd found the divine perspective on those who hated him. By their malice, he'd concluded, they had helped him "to count the world as nothing," to set his heart on God alone. And so he had prayed: "Give me grace, good Lord ... to think my greatest enemies my best friends."

St. Andrew Bobola

The Protestant Reformation wasn't the first major schism in the history of the Church. Another split, equally serious, had occurred five centuries before in 1054, when the churches of the East had separated from Rome. Reasons for the break were complex. Countless cultural and political factors had contributed, and in the intervening centuries, the same factors had sometimes led to violence, engendering bitterness and hatred that festered across the generations.

Given these historical realities, Polish Catholics in the seventeenth century were in a particularly precarious situation. Their nation's geography situated it in a religious borderland where the Eastern Orthodox and Western Latin churches overlapped. Though Catholics predominated in western Poland, in certain eastern parts of the country the majority of the population was Russian Orthodox. Many Catholics in the area had joined that communion because they lacked their own priests and churches. In recent years, however, the Jesuits had worked to reestablish Catholic parishes and bring about a number of reconversions, to the annoyance of the Orthodox hierarchy.

The result was an ecclesiastical battlefield. Despite the 1596 agreement of the Union of Brest-Litovsk, which had declared that the Roman and Russian churches would coexist peacefully, tensions simmered and often boiled over into open conflict. To make matters worse, in the mid-seventeenth century Russia and Poland were at war, and Cossack mercenaries in the service of the Russian czar made excursions into Polish territory. Many of these marauders had no religion at all, but some claimed the Orthodox faith, and with the encouragement of the Russians and some of the Orthodox clergy, they sought to drive the Catholics out of the land.

Capture and Martyrdom

In 1622 a young Polish Jesuit named Andrew Bobola was ordained in the city of Vilnius. He quietly served as a parish priest for most of the following thirty-three years. Twice he survived the dangerous ministry of caring for contagious victims of the plague, and he was well known for recruiting laypeople to help in visiting prisoners, caring for the poor, and catechizing children.[6]

When the czar's army sacked Vilnius in 1655, Fr. Andrew was unable to continue his ministry there. He therefore returned to the city of Pinsk, where some years earlier he'd served the minority Catholic population. Under the influence of his preaching, many former Catholics, including two entire villages in the area, returned to the Catholic faith. Not surprisingly, his success earned him the enmity of local Orthodox Christians; they dubbed him the "soul hunter."

In May of 1657, while Fr. Andrew was visiting another town, the Cossacks massacred the Catholics and Jews of a nearby village and occupied Pinsk. Orthodox informers told the soldiers where to find the priest, and soon they had captured him. He knew what kind of torment lay ahead; the Cossacks were infamous for their torture of Jesuit priests.

First, they tried with threats to make him go over to the Orthodox Church. When he refused, they stripped him and tied him to a tree, where they scourged him and knocked out several of his teeth. Then they set a crown of twigs on his head, tied him between two horses, and dragged him to another town, two miles away.

Once they arrived, one of the soldiers struck at Fr. Andrew's head with his sword, but he instinctively raised his hand against the blow, and three of his fingers were severed instead. The Cossacks dragged him into a butcher shop, stretched him out on a table, and demanded once more that he renounce his faith. He remained adamant, so the tortures continued.

Torches were applied to various parts of his body. Wood splinters were forced under his nails until his fingers split open. His tormentors peeled off the skin from his hands and scalp, then tore it from his chest and back to make for him, as they said mockingly, "a better chasuble."

They cut off his nose, lips, and thumbs, as well as his left index finger. Holes were cut into the palms of his hands. Through all these agonies, they kept shouting, "Deny your faith!"

Instead, the priest said gently, "Rather, you should be converted. My dear sons, what are you doing? May God be with you and convert your hearts from your anger."[7]

At those words, their rage exploded. They cut out his tongue to silence him.

For more than two hours their fury continued. They drove a butcher's awl through his chest, and tying his feet together, they hung him upside down from a butcher's hook. Finally, they beheaded him, and at last his passion was complete.

But his ministry to the Poles was not. After the saint went on to his reward, miraculous cures attributed to his intercession were reported throughout the land. At one point the pharmacists in Pinsk complained that St. Andrew had put their businesses in jeopardy—so many people were obtaining remedies from him instead of from their medicines!

A Promise of Freedom

The Poles have suffered terribly at the hands of other peoples since the days of St. Andrew. In the eighteenth century, powerful neighboring nations divided up and oppressed their land. More than a century passed before Poland finally became an independent nation again in 1918. Then German and Russian occupation in the World War II years and the Communist government established after the war made most of the twentieth century yet another nightmare for the Polish people, especially Polish Catholics.

Nevertheless, in 1819—at a time when Poland had no independent existence as a nation—St. Andrew had appeared to a Dominican priest, promising that one day, through God's mercy, Poland would be free. That promise lay buried under the heel of the oppressor, waiting to germinate, until 1990. Then the Polish Communist regime, largely through the heroic opposition of the Catholic Church, came at last to an end.

Today, despite many continuing political and spiritual challenges, Poland is indeed free, and St. Andrew Bobola is venerated as one of the nation's patron saints. In more ways than one, it seems, the blood of the martyrs continues to prove itself seed.

SEVEN

"LONG LIVE CHRIST THE KING!"
Martyrs of the Twentieth Century

They will make war on the Lamb, and the Lamb will conquer them, for he is Lord of lords and King of kings, and those with him are called and chosen and faithful.

REVELATION 17:14

Viva Cristo Rey! *Long live Christ the King!*

Blessed Miguel Pro,
last words as he faced the firing squad

There is no God here in the camp."

With these grim words, one of the barracks leaders at the Nazi camp in Dachau greeted the new arrivals. In a sense, this prisoner summed up the political ideology that has come to be responsible, in one form or another, for millions of Christian martyrdoms in the twentieth century. The Socialist dictators of Mexico ... the Republicans of the Spanish Civil War ... the Nazis of the German Third Reich ... the multiple Communist regimes and revolutionary groups from Russia to Cuba, from China to the Philippines ... all these have found their anti-Christian animus in atheism.

Such "godless messianic systems that tried to take the place of Christian hope," Pope John Paul II recently told a World

Youth Day gathering, "have shown themselves to be truly horrendous."[1] He should know—for much of his life he had to live under the oppressive control of Nazis or Communists.

A world without God is not only a world with false hope. It's also a world with a vacuum of authority, of morality, and ultimately of truth. The atheist political systems seek to exploit such a vacuum by enthroning the state within the individual soul, where only God has the right to rule. In these systems, the state claims to embody ultimate authority: What it declares to be right must be accepted as right; what it proclaims to be true must be accepted as true. All dissent must be silenced and destroyed.

A careful reading of the works of Karl Marx, for example, reveals alongside his economic analysis a near-religious mythology that has been rightly called a "secular messianism," in which Communism serves as Messiah. Having discarded all religion as fantasy, Marx prophesies the coming of a Communist millennium, a kind of kingdom of heaven whose "heaven" has no God. Yet we need only survey the social, cultural, spiritual, and even economic devastation of the lands where Marxism has had free reign to recognize how perversely destructive it is of all that is sane and human. Modern critics of the Church who condemn the casualties of the Inquisition should remember the observation of Soviet dissident Vladimir Bukovsky: Communism has typically killed as many people in one day as the Inquisition killed throughout all the hundreds of years of its existence.

History amply demonstrates that governments have always lusted to extend their dominion in one way or another. Like shipwrecked sailors trying to relieve their parched throats with saltwater—only to burn more fiercely after the draught—rulers who drink deeply of power only sharpen their thirst for more power still. Even so, the twentieth-century totalitarian states, whether Socialist, Fascist, Communist, or otherwise, have gone far beyond their political predecessors in this regard. They have embodied most diabolically this arrogant, merciless reach for complete control over human thought as well as behavior. And they have killed more Christians in the process than all the governments of all the nineteen centuries before them.

No doubt Christian failings have helped to provoke or intensify some modern attacks on the Church. In some cases, historical wrongs perpetrated by those who claimed the name of Christ—especially ungodly alliances of Christians with oppressive power structures—have planted the seeds of bitterness, doubt, and despair. When the poor, especially, lose faith in the Church as Christ's servant to be their advocate and protector, they grow vulnerable to the seductions of false messiahs who promise a utopia they can never deliver. They may then be tempted to avenge themselves on anyone, however personally innocent, who represents to them the faith they have abandoned.

Nevertheless, the murder of so many millions has been driven by something more than simple bitterness. Denying God, these atheistic revolutionaries and regimes have sought to crush the Church because of what the Church is by its very nature: a witness to the Reality that exposes their ideologies as lies and rejects their claim to ultimate authority and control.

Blessed Miguel Pro

Since the sixteenth-century conversion of millions of Native Americans through the help of Our Lady of Guadalupe, Mexico has been a largely Catholic land. Even so, the Church there has suffered from the nation's troubled political history ever since the country's independence from Spain. Like many revolutionaries before and after them, a number of Mexican leaders of the nineteenth and twentieth centuries hoped to replace, in only a short time, a corrupt and oppressive political system with a new way of life full of liberty, justice, and prosperity. Sadly—and again like so many other revolutionaries—they found themselves simply trading one gang of corrupt oppressors for another.

With the establishment of Mexico's first constitution as an independent nation in 1857, under the dictatorship of Benito Juarez, the Catholic Church was stripped of considerable power and possessions. In the following century, believers experienced at best some periods of uncomfortable peace with the government, at worst some virulent attacks intended to wipe out the Church altogether. Especially after the 1917 Revolution, which established the world's first socialist constitution (even before the one in Russia), Mexican Catholics suffered a number of outrages.

The authorities demolished, seized, and desecrated churches and other religious buildings—even private homes used for religious meetings were sometimes confiscated. Sacred vessels, sacramentals, and sacred works of art were destroyed or profaned. Many of the faithful were denied the sacraments because priests had to be licensed, and the government denied licenses to all but a few. Religious activities were confined to churches, if allowed at all. Religious orders were banned, as was religious instruction.

The situation was particularly difficult for Catholics in the state of Tabasco, ruled by a governor who had named his children Lucifer, Satan, and Lenin. He attempted to destroy all the churches and ordered all priests to marry, banishing any who refused. Most of the priests resisted and were expelled from the state, leaving behind only a few fugitive clergymen ministering in secret.

The people had a legitimate right to self-defense against the government forces that slaughtered so many of them and destroyed their churches and religious charitable institutions. Some did, in fact, take up arms; they called themselves the *Cristeros* and their uprising the *Cristiada*. Yet even though the government claimed the Church was promoting rebellion, the Catholic hierarchy both in Mexico and in Rome refrained from endorsing the rebels, calling on Catholics to seek peaceful means for change instead.

Echoing Tertullian's words about blood as seed, one Mexican bishop spoke of the Church's stand this way: "We cannot be responsible before God and man for bloodshed. Better that we should die, and that out of the martyrs' blood should come a new growth—as it is certain to come."[2] Among those who died, perhaps none has fertilized the growth of the Church in Mexico more than a young Jesuit named Miguel Agustin Pro.[3]

Early Life

Miguel was born to a middle-class family in 1891 in the village of Guadalupe in central Mexico. His father, Miguel Sr., was a mining engineer who homeschooled the boy through much of his childhood. His mother, Josefa, worked at home, caring for ten children, seven of whom survived to adulthood. Apparently, her dear Miguelito kept her busy; while still a toddler, we're told, the active little child escaped from his nursemaid and crawled out on a window ledge, three stories high, over a busy street, where his terrified Mama found and rescued him.

The boy was not an exceptional student in most subjects, but he and his siblings showed considerable musical talent, learning to play several instruments and forming an ensemble that performed at local events under Miguel's direction. Music remained a lifelong pleasure for him: Many years later, not long before his death, he jokingly promised a friend that when he went to heaven, he would cheer up any dour-faced saints he met there by performing a lively Mexican hat dance!

Humor was, in fact, a trademark of this playful priest-to-be. Practical jokes were his specialty, usually played on his sisters. Once, while on a stroll with his favorite, Concepcion, he dashed to the door of a house they were passing and knocked until the man of the house—a total stranger to them—answered. Miguel explained, to his sister's horror, that she wanted to buy the beautiful statue of the Virgin Mary that stood in his window. It was, she later told her parents, the ugliest, most gaudy statue she'd ever laid eyes upon. She was relieved when the gentleman refused to sell it—it was a family treasure, he insisted. But Miguel enjoyed the prank all the same.

Miguel's family, especially his mother, were devout Catholics, attending Mass regularly, receiving Confession and Communion frequently, praying the family Rosary together. Yet in his early years Miguel seems to have had no special interest in religion. He adamantly refused, for example, to become an acolyte.

As a child he sometimes carried water and candies to the miners who worked with his father. In his teen years he went to work at the mining office. These experiences later led him to read deeply in Catholic analyses of modern social problems and prepared him well for work among laborers, who were often tempted to take up the Socialist banner. His mother founded and operated a hospital for the miners, providing him a role model of concern for the adverse and unjust circumstances they often endured.

During his three years at the mine, Miguel grew restless and uncharacteristically moody. The young man seems to have been wrestling with God: He stopped attending Mass for a while and was the only member of his family not to receive Communion when his oldest sister, Maria de la Luz, entered a convent in 1911. When Maria was joined there soon after by Concepcion, Miguel was brought to tears, commenting that "the heavens had fallen" on his head.[4]

Not only did he feel the bitterness of losing the companionship of two beloved sisters; he apparently was resisting the call to a vocation himself. Miguel was attached to a non-Catholic girlfriend, but Providence had other plans. One day he mistakenly mailed to his mother a letter intended for his girlfriend, and the letter written to his mother he sent instead to the señorita. That error ultimately caused an end to the romance.

Entering Religious Life

At last giving up all resistance to his vocation, at the age of twenty he entered the Jesuit novitiate. Miguel was known for organizing outings and sports for his colleagues there. He continued to play the guitar, sing, and dance for their entertainment. Yet the young man displayed an earnest, disciplined side as well; his fellow Jesuits noted that he was convinced God wanted him to be a saint.

The revolution had begun just before he entered the seminary, and all around, conditions were worsening. Roving militias, claiming political agendas but acting more like bandits, were looting and destroying churches, schools, businesses, railroad stations, and government buildings. Priests were frequently subjected to torture, mutilation, and murder. Religious communities were held hostage; often the men were exiled and the women raped. Those executed for various "crimes" against the state could be seen hanging from telegraph posts.

On August 5, 1914, soldiers ransacked the novitiate's main

house and burned the library. More violence was certain to come, so the rector sent the men out in small groups, dressed in street clothes, to find their way, on foot and by train, to Laredo, Texas.

Miguel made his way disguised as a rancher, first to Zamora, then to Guadalajara. The trek was extremely dangerous. In each of these towns, local officials ordered all the priests to be rounded up, and on the road the Jesuits had to evade soldiers and sleep in cornfields. At Guadalajara, the cathedral had been turned into an army barracks, where profane soldiers desecrated whatever religious articles and art they could find.

Before Miguel's exile, God granted him a great favor: Because his family had moved to Guadalajara, he was able to say goodbye. It was the last time he would see his mother.

In many ways, the young man's journey began only when he reached Texas. From there he went on to California, down to Nicaragua, through the Panama Canal, and across the ocean to Spain and then Belgium. After considerable study and training, he was at last ordained in Belgium on August 31, 1925.

While studying Catholic social philosophy there, Fr. Pro developed a deeper understanding of his nation's problems. He concluded that Socialism, despite its fatal errors as a political system and its opposition to the Church, sometimes displayed genuinely good intentions—intentions that Catholics should share. "The Socialists," he wrote, "are more interested in the fate of the workers than we are. The popular masses know this.... We ought to talk, to shout against injustices."[5]

Meanwhile, Fr. Miguel had developed a severe stomach ailment that required multiple surgeries—one of which involved the removal of large portions of his stomach without any anesthesia. When his health failed to improve, his superiors sent him home to Mexico in 1926, hoping that a more familiar climate and cuisine might help. Perhaps they didn't realize just how ruthless the persecution there had become. Plutarco Elias Calles had come to power as president—the tyrant dubbed the "Mexican Nero" because of his passionate, diabolical hatred for the Church. All priests had been banned from the country.

Nevertheless, Fr. Pro believed that his personal mission was to invest his life in taking the gospel to his countrymen, so he eagerly accepted the assignment. After slipping through customs undetected as a priest—a near-miracle in itself—Fr. Pro reported for duty in Mexico City.

Back in Mexico

Less than a month later, the Calles government decreed a suspension of all public worship. All priests were subject to arrest and prosecution. Fr. Miguel was unknown in the capital city, so he ministered secretly in several parishes, riding his bike in secular clothing to administer the sacraments and to collect and distribute material goods for the poor.

Despite the government's threats, up to fifteen hundred of the faithful were soon meeting him at hidden "Communion stations" around the city. On a typical day hearing confessions, he would begin at 5:50 A.M. and continue for up to fourteen hours straight. A number of Socialists were converted. In addition to such priestly responsibilities, no fewer than ninety-six families came to be dependent on him for their daily food.

For a while, the young priest was able to escape detection, though he narrowly escaped arrest several times and had to outwit his enemies. Finally an order went out for his arrest, and he had to go into hiding. Everywhere the authorities were preying on both priests and lay leaders: They were tortured, dragged behind vehicles, shot while celebrating Mass, hung, thrown from trains. Many simply joined the ranks of the *desaparecidos*, never heard from again.

During this difficult time, the young man's acting skills saved him more than once. Fr. Pro became a master of disguises. Dressed as a mechanic one day, he talked to a group of chauffeurs; the nearby police had no clue that he was preaching. One morning when he arrived at a designated meeting place to find police detectives waiting, he pretended to flash a badge and said, "There's a cat [police slang for a priest in hiding] inside there!" The detectives thought he was an undercover agent and let him pass. After he fulfilled his duties, he left, in full view of the police, who saluted respectfully.

On yet another occasion, the police were closing in on him, barely fifty yards away. He saw a girl walk by—a total stranger—linked arms with her, and whispered, "Help me; I'm a priest." She proved a fine actress herself, pretending to be his girlfriend, and the police who were searching for him passed by the "lovers" without a second thought.

Each time he evaded the police and was out of danger, Fr. Miguel wrote to his superior, he and his comrades actually thought of the work as fun—life in disguise, he noted, was the life of a comedian. Despite the adversities he faced, Fr. Miguel's sense of humor clearly remained intact. One day he even posed for a smiling photograph in civilian disguise, smoking a cigar, right in front of the home of the dreaded President Calles!

Arrest and Execution

Nevertheless, the terror intensified. In the first week of October 1927 alone, an estimated three hundred political assassinations were carried out by the Calles regime. Fire hoses and even guns were turned on elderly women praying in churches. Printing religious literature or teaching religion led to accusations of sedition. False charges, confiscations, and demands for bribes multiplied. Mexico had become utterly lawless.

Then, on November 13, a bomb was tossed at a car driven by the president-elect, a man closely aligned with Calles. His bodyguards apprehended the assailants and the vehicle they were driving. One of them confessed to having planned the attack alone. Yet the police looked for more suspects.

The would-be assassins' car had once been owned by Fr. Miguel's brother Humberto. All the Pro brothers had solid alibis backed up by witnesses, but on November 18 the authorities arrested three of them anyway——Miguel, Humberto, and Roberto—along with other "suspects." Miguel was never even questioned about his role in the affair; he was simply presumed to be guilty. No evidence was offered of any wrongdoing by any of the men.

Public protests multiplied while the men were held in prison, but to no avail. Without even the pretense of a trial, Calles ordered the prisoners to be executed by firing squad. Thinking to make of them a public example—or perhaps hoping that the priest would plead for mercy—he invited journalists and photographers from all over the nation and the world to attend the event.

On the morning of the executions, November 23, a lawyer convinced a local judge to sign a stay of execution; the lawyer, however, was locked out of the proceedings. A last-minute appeal from the Argentine ambassador earned the youngest brother, Roberto, a reprieve. But it was too late to save the others.

The authorities kept the order of execution a secret from the prisoners themselves. They realized their fate only in their last minutes as they were being led out to face the firing squad. But the young priest was well prepared to meet his destiny.

Some weeks before, he had prayed to the Blessed Virgin of Sorrows: "I covet the jeers and mockery of Calvary; the slow agony of your Son, the contempt, the ignominy, the infamy of his Cross. I wish to stand at your side, most sorrowful Virgin, strengthening my spirit with your tears, consummating my sacrifice with your martyrdom, sustaining my heart with your solitude, loving my God and your God with the immolation of my being."[6]

Then, just a few days before his arrest, he'd celebrated Mass at a local convent and told the Mother Superior afterward: "I offered my life for the saving of Mexico some time ago, Sister, and this morning at Mass I felt that God had accepted it."[7]

One of the policemen who had hunted him down was among those who led him out of the jail cell to his death. On the way, the man turned and begged the priest's forgiveness. Fr. Pro put his arm around the trembling man to comfort him and said, "You have not only my forgiveness, but my thanks." He extended the same grace to the firing squad, saying softly, "May God forgive you all."[8]

Fr. Miguel was granted, as a last request, permission to pray. He knelt, drew from his pocket a Rosary and a crucifix, kissed the crucifix, and prayed earnestly, lifting his eyes to heaven. Then he stood to face his executioners, kissing the crucifix once more, holding it in his right hand and the Rosary in his left. Refusing the traditional blindfold, he stretched out his arms in the shape of a cross and said firmly, clearly, *"Viva Cristo Rey!"* "Long live Christ the King!"

The soldiers fired, mortally wounding him, but he lay on the ground, still breathing. The general in charge walked over to him, put a revolver to his head, and finished the deed.

"Dealing Out Favors"

Calles' plan to manipulate the press for his anti-Catholic political agenda backfired. Photographs of the execution were quickly and widely distributed, becoming objects of devotion to thousands of the faithful. The government declared it a crime to possess them, but nothing could stop their circulation.

The Pro brothers' bodies were returned to the family home for viewing. When one of their sisters wept bitterly, Miguel Sr. asked her, "Is this how you behave in the presence of a saint?" People filed by the caskets all night—laborers and professionals, men and women, even half a dozen government agents came in to kneel and pray.

Before he died Fr. Pro told a friend, "If I'm ever caught, get ready to ask me for things when I'm in heaven." The martyr promised to "deal out favors like a deck of cards."[9] He wasted no time in fulfilling his promise. An elderly blind woman who came to touch his body at the funeral received her sight. Within a week, three others had testified to his help.

The day of the funeral, tens of thousands of mourners lined the streets to watch the procession of about five hundred cars. The government had forbidden all public demonstrations in honor of the martyrs, but the people were defiant. Many dark days still lay ahead for the Church in Mexico, yet the courageous example of Fr. Miguel would give hope and strength to millions. As the coffins were carried through the streets, everywhere the crowd took up the chant:

"Viva Cristo Rey!"[10]

The Catholic Church and the Nazi Holocaust

If ever the spirit of antichrist reared its head in modern times, the world saw it in the face of Adolf Hitler. The volumes detailing and analyzing Nazi atrocities would fill a large library, yet the story could never be fully told in all its gruesome details. In the horrors of the Third Reich, we see with utter clarity hell's hatred both of God's ancient chosen people, the Jews, and of their spiritual descendants, the Church. Sadly enough, in one of the bitter ironies of history, many European Christians themselves had cultivated the anti-Semitic roots that helped to provide the Nazis with such demonic vitality.

Though the Reich openly declared war on the Jewish people, its attacks on the Catholic Church were hidden behind public posturings of toleration intended to deceive the German people and the rest of the world about the Führer's plans. "The evil that's gnawing at our vitals is our priests," Hitler once ranted privately to his henchmen. "The time will come when I settle my accounts with them, and I'll go straight to the point. In less than ten years from now, things will have quite another look— I can promise them."[11]

While Pope Pius XII and other Vatican officials worked behind the scenes to oppose the madness, the Nazi machine pressed violently against the clergy, religious, and laymen and women who dared to oppose it. Only scanty information has survived about the total numbers of men and women religious who suffered, and some dioceses were unable to maintain as complete a documentation as others. Yet even the incomplete records reveal a staggering assault against the Church.[12]

Between 1933 and 1945, more than eight thousand clergy— comprising more than a third of the diocesan clergy and nearly a fifth of the male religious in 1937—were subjected to nearly twenty-three thousand punishments, ranging from interrogation to execution. Four hundred and eighteen German priests were sent to concentration camps, and this includes a count of German priests only; the Dachau camp alone held nearly 2,600 Catholic priests, many of whom came from Poland.

Why did Hitler hate the Church? The revolutionaries of eighteenth-century France and twentieth-century Mexico, Spain, and Russia claimed to be avenging themselves on Christian leaders who had helped maintain an oppressive status quo that the rebels sought to overthrow. Yet no such claim could be made in twentieth-century Germany. Instead, the clash between the Führer and the Church had a more immediate origin: Hitler knew that the Church stood in the way of his diabolical plans to amass unprecedented power and to annihilate or subjugate millions of innocent people. Aryan ideology, with its idolatry of race and power, was anathema to Catholic moral teaching.

St. Teresa Benedicta (Edith Stine), Jewish Catholic

Nazism's two great hatreds—of the Jews and of the Church—converged tragically on a brilliant young German woman named Edith Stein. Edith was born to Jewish parents on October 12, 1891—*Yom Kippur,* the Day of Atonement, one of the Jewish calendar's holiest days. Unlike many German Jews of the time, the Steins strictly observed Jewish law in their home in what was then Breslau, Germany, now Wroclaw, Poland.[13]

Her father, Siegfried, ran a successful lumber business, and the family's relative prosperity allowed them the luxury of enjoying the best of German culture. However, Siegfried died when Edith was only three. Her mother, Auguste, was left with the little girl and ten other, older children to rear.

Early on, Edith displayed a fierce intellect, a remarkable memory, and a thirst for learning. After a short stint in kindergarten, she refused to continue the class because she was so far ahead of the other students. The headmaster of her grammar school later summed up her abilities by quoting an old German proverb as a pun on her name: "Strike the stone [in German, *Stein*], and wisdom will leap forth."[14]

Scoring high marks in all her subjects of study except mathematics, she turned her attention to a wide range of fields. After a disappointing and consequently brief season of studying psychology at the University of Breslau, she decided to focus instead on philosophy. Stein was especially attracted by the phenomenologist school of philosophy represented by Edmund Husserl, so in 1913 she enrolled at the University of Goettingen to study with him.

Her studies there, culminating in a doctorate awarded *summa cum laude* when she was twenty-five, began to challenge some of her assumptions about the world and about herself. The meaning of the human person conceived as a living whole came to occupy her attention. Tellingly, she chose for her dissertation the topic of how empathy for another human being is possible.

A Spiritual Journey

Even in childhood, Edith had shown something of a contemplative character. Because of her occasional mysterious silences, her sisters dubbed her, using scriptural imagery, "a book with seven seals." Perhaps such intense times of reflection allowed her opportunity to question her family's faith. In any case, when she was about thirteen, she stopped praying, and until she was almost twenty-one, she doubted God's existence.

Her teacher Husserl insisted, however, that even agnostics could not afford to neglect the study of religion as a significant human phenomenon. Though he himself didn't profess Christian faith in those years, his approach to philosophy led some of his students to become Christians. Even before his own conversion, he once joked that the Church should canonize him for making so many converts. Meanwhile, Stein was becoming friends at the university with Christians whose lives influenced her deeply.

Among them was a convert to Lutheranism, Adolf Reinach, Husserl's personal assistant. Stein later observed that she could never "remember meeting anyone so absolutely good-hearted." The love he showed her, even as a stranger, became her "first glimpse into a totally new world."[15]

When Reinach died in 1917 at the Battle of Flanders Field in World War I, Stein was devastated. She went to visit his widow, by then also a close friend. Instead of finding her, as she'd expected, deeply in despair, however, the grieving woman displayed a confident hope in the resurrection and spent her time comforting those who had come to comfort her.

"It was my first encounter with the Cross," Stein later wrote, "and the divine power it bestows on those who carry it. For the first time, I was seeing with my very eyes the Church, born from its Redeemer's sufferings, triumphant over the sting of death. That was the moment my unbelief collapsed and Christ shone forth—in the mystery of the Cross."[16]

Stein stayed on at the university for a while after graduation to assist Husserl in his work, but eventually she returned to Breslau. Exhausted and emptied by the extended demands of her university labors, she entered a dark season of struggle, when she seemed unable to think or even to love as she should. Even so, in time she sensed a new energy flowing into her soul from outside herself—though she wasn't at all certain about its Source.

Merely philosophical texts lacked what she was searching for. One night at a friend's house in the summer of 1921, Stein took from the bookshelf a copy of St. Teresa of Avila's autobiography. From the first page, she was hooked. She stayed up all night reading to finish the volume, and the next morning she remarked, "That is truth."

Stein right away bought a catechism and missal and began

her self-instruction in the Catholic faith. Immediately after she attended her first Mass, she followed the priest out of the church and asked him to baptize her. He asked her what kind of instruction she'd had; she simply smiled and invited him to examine her knowledge of the faith. The priest did just that and was impressed by what he heard. He agreed to baptize her, but not until the following New Year's Day, 1922.

Not surprisingly, Auguste Stein was devastated by the news of her daughter's conversion. Even after her baptism, the wayward child still accompanied her mother to synagogue on Saturdays, but those visits would never again be the same. Now when the ancient Jewish Scriptures were read publicly, Edith heard in them a new Voice.

"You don't know what it means to me," she later told an acquaintance, "to be a daughter of the chosen people—to belong to Christ, not only spiritually, but according to the flesh."[17]

New Horizons

Stein may have begun thinking about becoming a Carmelite at this time, but the timing wasn't right: Her mother needed time to work through her grief, and most convents probably wouldn't have accepted so recent a convert anyway. Stein's new spiritual director believed that her intellectual gifts had a contribution to make to the Church, so for the time being he recommended her for a teaching post at a Dominican school in Speyer.

Teaching German may not have presented her with much of an intellectual challenge. Yet she showed an intense interest in her students, offering extra academic and personal help and showing small kindnesses to the girls who were lonely or homesick. She also took on regular work with the poor. Soon Stein found her prayer life expanding and deepening. Sometimes she would spend hours before the Blessed Sacrament.

Meanwhile, other doors were opening. The Jesuit scholar Erich Przywara, whom she met at Speyer, recognized Stein's gifts and persuaded her to translate into German Cardinal John Newman's *Letters and Journals*. Next he talked her into translating St. Thomas Aquinas' *Quaestiones Disputatae de Veritate* (*Disputed Questions on Truth*).

If his intention was to introduce her to some of the riches of Thomist philosophy, he succeeded. In the days to come her new philosophical works would offer comparisons between the thought of Aquinas and that of her old master, Husserl. The penetrating insights of the medieval Dominican friar were now challenging and enriching her philosophical perspectives, as well as her faith.

Przywara arranged for her to lecture at Catholic institutions across Germany. On these occasions, Stein often spoke of the special problems encountered by women in modern societies. She insisted that women had a unique role as mothers, but she also recognized that they were taking on new and wider roles in society as well, roles that made difficult demands on them. "More than anything else today," she concluded, "what is needed is the baptism of spirit and fire. This alone can prepare those who shape human life to take their rightful place at the front lines in the great battle between Christ and Lucifer."[18]

Edith returned home to Breslau to live with her mother, and sought to secure a university teaching post. However, the way was blocked for several reasons. Neither Thomism nor phenomenology were popular in the German academy at that time. Women were less likely to be hired for such positions. And growing anti-Semitism all but ruled her out as a candidate to teach. In the spring of 1932, she finally accepted a lectureship at the Catholic Educational Institute in Muenster. Soon afterward, however, she was quietly asked to step down until public sentiment toward Jews became less worrisome.

In the spring of 1933 Stein at last resolved to enter the Carmel. She was accepted as a postulant at Cologne and was clothed there in 1934. Though she continued her writing, most of her time was spent in the unfamiliar and humbling routine of manual labor assigned to the novices.

A Share in Christ's Passion

All across Germany, the political situation deteriorated rapidly. Already Sister Teresa Benedicta of the Cross (the name Stein took) seemed to have a sense that she would take part in the drama unfolding beyond the walls of the cloister. When she'd first spoken with the prioress about joining the community, she'd summed up conditions in Germany this way: "Human activity can't help us, but only the passion of Christ. My desire is to share in that."[19]

On the day of her profession, a friend had noted with relief that now, despite her Jewish ancestry, Stein would be safe. "I don't think so," she replied. "They will surely take me out of here."[20]

By 1938, her prediction seemed certain to come true. Religious houses were being closed. The authorities in Cologne had taken note that "Dr. Edith Stein" of the Carmel was Jewish. After November 8, the infamous *Kristallnacht*—when Jewish homes, businesses, and synagogues were attacked throughout the nation—no one could any longer entertain doubts about the Nazis' intentions. Edith remarked, "This is the shadow of the Cross falling on my people."[21]

Her prioress realized that even Jewish Christians were no longer safe in Germany. Sister Teresa Benedicta was thus sent to the Carmel in Echt, the Netherlands, on December 31. Yet she knew that she was still within the reach of her enemies, and she prepared herself for the horrors she expected to come sooner or later.

"Please," she wrote the prioress on Passion Sunday, 1939, "may your Reverence allow me to offer myself to the Heart of Jesus as a sacrifice of expiation for true peace: that the reign of the Antichrist may perish."[22] She prayed fervently that her life and death would be accepted by God as an offering for the sake of the Jewish people, "that the Lord may be received by his own and his kingdom come in glory."[23]

In 1940 Edith's sister Rosa, who had by now also become Catholic, came to Echt to live in a room of the convent outside the enclosure. That year the Germans invaded Holland, and the sisters sought asylum in a Carmel in Switzerland. The Swiss convent had room to receive Edith as a professed member, but it was too crowded for Rosa. Edith refused to leave Rosa behind, and both remained at Echt.

On July 26, 1942, the Archbishop of Utrecht ordered that a pastoral letter be read in all the parishes of the Netherlands protesting the deportation of the Jews to camps and other outrages. A week later, in retaliation for this and other statements of opposition by Christian leaders, the Nazis rounded up all Catholics of Jewish background and sent them to the camps.[24]

The Stein sisters were among those taken to the train station to be deported—first to the main holding camp at Amersfoort, then to the central detention camp at Westerbork, and finally on to Auschwitz, Poland. We know little about their final days, but in one brief note Edith was able to send to the sisters at Echt, she reported: "I am content about everything.... *Ave crux, spes unica* [Hail to the Cross, our only hope]."

A few days later, Sister Teresa Benedicta of the Cross and her sister died in the gas chambers at Auschwitz: a sacrifice offered on behalf of her people, her nation, the Church, and the world.

The day was *Tish'a B'ab* on the Jewish calendar, a traditional day of mourning for the destruction of the two ancient Jewish temples. To the Reich they were no more than a statistic in the efforts to annihilate the Jews and destroy the Church. But the Nazis were quite mistaken.

"In the solitary conversation of consecrated souls," Sister Teresa Benedicta had once written, "there are prepared those widely visible events of the Church's history that renew the face of the earth.... And our own time, seeing that all else fails, finds itself more and more urged to hope for ultimate salvation from these hidden sources."[25] In this brave saint, another seed had been planted in secret, with the promise of a harvest to come.[26]

The Catholic Church and Communism

The Nazis saw the Catholic Church as an obstacle to be crushed and its fragments swept away. The Communists, on the other hand, have viewed Catholic faith—indeed, religion of any kind—as a deadly disease to be exterminated at all costs. Not surprisingly, for most of a century now they have pursued a perverse and ruthless policy of terror and violence in their attempt to wipe out even the memory of the name of Christ.

Every weapon at the disposal of a powerful totalitarian state has been used by Communists against the Christians: destruction or confiscation of church property and suspension or control of church activities; bans on religious education and literature, with forced indoctrination of children; disinformation campaigns and ubiquitous propaganda; secret police, informants, and infiltrators; arrests, disappearances, and imprisonments; interrogation, brainwashing, and torture; concentration camps, slave labor, and executions.

The "Opiate of the People"?

Karl Marx, whose economic and political dogmas provided much of the foundation for Communist and socialist thought and policy, dismissed religion contemptuously as "the opiate of the people." Faith, he insisted, was a numbing drug prescribed for the ignorant masses, so they wouldn't feel enough pain to provoke a revolution. They would no longer want or need such fantasies, he boasted, once they embraced his superior vision of history. Yet Marx's disciples found, as they sought to realize his ideas in concrete historical settings, that Jesus Christ was not so easily dismissed.

The Church in Communist lands has suffered horribly at the hands of atheist governments. Official church statistics show the severity of the attack, for example, on the Byzantinerite Catholics in the Ukraine. In 1946, the Ukrainian Catholic Church was thriving. It included four dioceses, eight bishops, 2,722 parishes, 4,119 churches and chapels, 142 monasteries and convents, 2,628 diocesan priests, 164 men religious, 773 women religious, 229 seminarians, and more than four million laypeople. By 1949, the Communist regime had reduced all of these numbers to zero.[27]

All Church and Church-related property had been confiscated or torn down. All public Church activities had been outlawed. All visible Church organizational structures had been suppressed. Religious communities were dissolved. Bishops, priests, religious, and many laypeople had been exiled, sent to prison camps, or worked to death in forced labor.

Of course, the Ukrainian Church didn't cease to exist, as much as its enemies might have wished it so. Much of the Catholic community represented by the earlier statistics went underground. Even in the hellish concentration camps, believers worshipped and prayed, the sacraments were administered, and priests were ordained by bishops—all in secret.

When the Communist powers throughout the Soviet bloc began to collapse toward the end of the century, the Catholic Church in the Ukraine at last came out of hiding, chastened and purified, but very much alive. After so many years of oppression, believers showed remarkable strength and vitality. There were eight bishops, about a thousand priests, twelve hundred women religious, and six religious orders. More than fifteen hundred Catholic congregations quickly formed. Once seminaries opened, candidates for the priesthood multiplied.

The heroic story of Catholic Ukraine's resurrection is dramatic, yet believers in other Communist lands could offer similar accounts of hope and heroism under extreme adversity. Marxists who have seized political power in nation after nation have expected to find in the Christian faith a dying illusion. Instead, they've encountered a vital, supernatural organism—one whose deep roots survive tenaciously in winter so that new shoots can burst forth energetically when at last the spring arrives.

Catholics in Vietnam

In Vietnam, the winter is not yet over. Once the Communists had decisively driven out the French colonial power from the North in 1954, they immediately began measures to root out the Catholic Church there. After the fall of Saigon in 1975, they predictably lost little time in extending the terror to include all the new territory that had come under their rule. The oppressive policies so familiar to believers in the North soon became a daily reality for those in the South as well.

Of course, persecution of the Church in Vietnam by no means began with the Communists. As a crossroads for many nations and peoples, the land has a long history of cultural conflict. Chinese invaders many centuries ago brought their way of life, including Confucianism; Indian traders later introduced Buddhism; European explorers and missionaries brought the Christian faith in the sixteenth century.

Relations between the Vietnamese rulers and the Church often depended on shifting political realities that had little to do with religion. Buddhists as well as Christians suffered martyrdoms from time to time. In the half century before Vietnam became a French protectorate in 1883, official opposition to Christianity intensified, with somewhere between one hundred thousand and three hundred thousand believers killed or otherwise persecuted.

With the coming of the Communists, however, the assault became systematic and sustained. About 1,120,000 Catholics lived in the North by that time; soon after, about 670,000 of them fled to the South. Those who remained—most of whom had no choice—descended into a nightmare of terror. Prominent clergy, religious, and lay leaders were harassed, arrested, and imprisoned. Catholic schools and other charitable institutions were closed or taken over. Christians who showed any sign of resistance were herded into "reeducation centers" and concentration camps.

Documented reports tell, for example, of young students in one school having chopsticks hammered into their ears by Communist soldiers—leaving them deaf—because they had listened to the teacher talk about religion. The teacher himself had his tongue cut out with a bayonet. One priest was accused of "treason" and had eight nails hammered into his head as a "crown of thorns." He was able to receive medical care in the South, but when he recovered, he courageously insisted on returning to his parish in the North.

Servant of God Marcel Van

Perhaps the story of a single Vietnamese martyr may serve as a representative and a memorial for all the other martyrs who have lost their lives under the global Communist onslaught against the Church. Servant of God Marcel Van was born in 1928 to a family of poor rice farmers in a small village between Hanoi and Haiphong. His parents raised him in the Catholic faith and he never left it, though he encountered a number of difficulties that might have led to despair in a less determined young man.[28]

From an early age he showed more than a common interest in religion, so his parents sent him off to work in a parish in the 1930s. A stubborn and sometimes eccentric child, he chafed under the arrangements.

To make matters worse, some of the priests and catechists he encountered abused him physically, and one catechist at the minor seminary even tried to abuse him sexually when he was only seven years old—threatening to bury him alive if he resisted. Other catechists beat him, tempted him to various sins, and taunted him for his devotion to God. Later, he found that some of the priests appointed to parishes where he studied were given to drunkenness, fornication, and other grave sins.

At the age of twelve Van finally ran away from his tormentors and took up living on the streets, surviving by his wits, occasional handouts, and sheer stubbornness. There were times when he was so hungry that he would eat the wax drippings off the altar candles in church. Once he narrowly escaped being sold into slavery.

Spiritual Growth
Miraculously, through all these trials Van's love for God and the Church remained firm. He finally found another parish to

accept him for religious training. Sadly, he found there some of the same kinds of moral and spiritual baseness that he'd seen before. Now, however, a new mission was crystalizing for him: He wanted to be a revolutionary.

The Communists at that time had already begun their resistance to the French presence. But Van didn't want to be a political activist. He sought to become a spiritual leader who could help to overthrow the corrupt conditions he'd encountered in the seminary and in parish life. He later recalled: "I wanted to be a revolutionary ... [in] the struggle ... to create a better future for the Church in Vietnam."[29]

After being transferred to another minor seminary, Van came across a copy of the famous autobiography of St. Thérèse of Lisieux, *Diary of a Soul*. Once he read it, he fell in love. She was the spiritual advisor he so desperately needed. Her "little way" offered him a path to God that even a former street urchin could walk. Van was fourteen then, and he never again was without a copy of that wise spiritual road map.

Then an intriguing spiritual development took place: Van began to talk with St. Thérèse—not simply addressing her in prayer, but also listening to her in two-way conversations. She comforted and counseled him, challenged and corrected him. The dialogues went on for years.

The saint's gentle wisdom brought him close to God in faith. Closeness to certain others, however, was another matter. Though wicked men had abused him, Van found it most difficult to forgive not them but the French. The Europeans had abused his country, and he hated them.

Once St. Thérèse asked the young man to pray for the French. "I can never pray for those wretched French colonialists!" he insisted. He might be willing to pray for the French missionary priests and nuns, he admitted, because they had been the fathers and mothers in the faith for the Vietnamese.

"But as far as the French colonialists are concerned, they can go to hell!" They had too much "cruelty and contempt" for his people. If he had a gun, he told the saint, he'd kill them, and he'd enjoy doing it.[30]

The saint agreed that the French—her own people—had sinned against the Vietnamese, and that the Asians had suffered greatly. Yet, instead of a gun, she replied, he should take up prayer as a weapon. He must pray for his enemies to be spiritually transformed.

The urgent need, she said, was "for someone to offer himself quietly in prayer and sacrifice." Only then could the two nations be reconciled, and "the power of evil ... brought to an end." Prayer and sacrifice were the only effective strategy for the spiritual revolution so desperately needed in Vietnam—and in France as well.[31]

Becoming a Redemptorist

Van had always wanted to be a priest, but St. Thérèse told him that God had other plans. He was to become a lay member of the Redemptorists in Hanoi. In this ministry, she warned, he would face severe testing, but Christ would be with him even in the darkest hours.

Now the young man began to have other mystical experiences. He received disturbing prophecies about the world's future. He engaged in conversations with Christ. At times he plunged into ecstasies in which he felt as if he were "disappearing into the heart of God." All this he carefully recorded.

When war broke out between the French and the Vietnamese Communists in 1945, Van left Hanoi, where the Communists had their strongest foothold, and flew to Saigon in the South. In 1952 he took his final vows with the Redemptorists there. Yet something was wrong. He grew restless.

In 1954 the nation was divided between North and South, with the Communists in control of the North. As hundreds of thousands of refugees fled south in terror to escape the northern regime, Van heard Jesus say that the young Redemptorist was to head north, to the people who needed him most.

He obeyed immediately and flew back into the heart of the raging political and spiritual storm. He arrived on September 14, the Feast of the Cross. In the midst of the Communists, Van noted, someone must be there who loved God.

Once settled, he returned to his spiritual work, hoping not to attract the attention of the authorities. In the marketplace one day, however, he couldn't resist openly challenging those whom the government had sent out to spread lies about the non-Communist government in the South. He was subsequently taken in for questioning.

The interrogations lasted for several days, from early morning till the middle of the night. The police demanded a "confession," but Van had nothing to confess. They urged him to join the Communist cause, but he refused. They claimed that he was having sex with a woman they knew, demanding that he break his religious vows and marry her. Van remained firm.

Next he was placed for five months in solitary confinement. Then came incarceration with other dissidents in Hanoi's central prison. Finally Van was sentenced to fifteen years' imprisonment for spreading propaganda against the government.

In the first concentration camp, the guards tried to "reeducate" him through brainwashing techniques, but to no avail. They offered him his freedom if he would only make an accusation against his religious superior, but he remained silent. His courage and endurance gave comfort and strength to the other prisoners, who sought out a man who could maintain in such dark circumstances what Van called "an indestructible joy."

Eventually he was transferred to a second, more brutal camp. There he was beaten and left in a dark cell for a full two years. For the last three months of his confinement, in early 1958, he was shackled and allowed no visitors.

By the time the isolation term had ended, Van's thin and weakened body was consumed with tuberculosis and beriberi. At last he gave up his stubborn spirit on June 10, 1959. He had brought to completion the mission God had given him, a mission he'd described once in a note smuggled out of prison to his superior. In Van's statement we can recognize the words of a true spiritual son of St. Thérèse.

"I," he had written, "am the victim of Love."[32]

EIGHT

"IN PERSECUTION THE CHURCH
BEGINS AND ENDS"
The Triumph of the Martyrs

I saw under the altar the souls of those who had been slain for the word of God and for the witness they had borne.... They were each given a white robe and told to rest a little longer, until the number of their fellow servants and their brethren should be complete, who were to be killed as they themselves had been.... The Lamb in the midst of the throne will be their shepherd, and he will guide them to springs of living water; and God will wipe away every tear from their eyes.

REVELATION 6:9, 11; 7:17

In persecution the Church begins and ends. [Christ] left her in persecution, and he will [return to] find her in persecution. He recognizes her as his own—he framed, and he will claim her—as a persecuted Church, bearing his Cross. And that awful relic of him which he gave her, and which she is found with at the end, she cannot have lost by the way.

Venerable John Cardinal Newman,
Advent Sermons on Antichrist, 4

Fatima. The very name of that once-obscure little Portuguese village has stirred debate all over the world ever since Our Lady's startling appearances there in 1917. Perhaps the most controversial element of the event involves what came to be known as the third part of the secret of Fatima, a prophetic message entrusted by the Virgin to three little children who were told that it couldn't be made public at the time.

Eventually, the first two portions of the vision were widely publicized, but the third remained a mystery known only to the visionaries themselves, the popes, and a handful of other Church officials. For decades, speculations, counterspeculations, and rumors abounded over the contents of that last part of the secret. Nor were all of these discussions laid to rest when the message was at last published, during the Jubilee year, by Pope John Paul II. Controversy continues to rage over the vision's correct interpretation; some Catholics dispute the contention of the Congregation for the Doctrine of the Faith that all the events described in the prophetic vision have already come to pass.

Whatever position they may take on the matter of past or future fulfillment, none can deny that the secret of Fatima offers a vivid depiction of massive Christian martyrdom. The description of Sr. Lucia dos Santos, the sole Fatima visionary still living, tells of "bishops, priests, men and women religious going up a steep mountain," toward an immense cross, led by the Holy Father. The way passes through a ruined city and alongside numerous corpses. When the pope at last reaches the foot of the cross and kneels to pray, he is "killed by a group of soldiers."[1]

"In the same way," she continues, "there died one after another the other bishops, priests, men and women religious, and various lay people of different ranks and positions. Beneath the two arms of the cross there were two angels each with a crystal aspersorium [the sprinkler used to apply holy water] in his hand, in which they gathered up the blood of the martyrs and with it sprinkled the souls that were making their way to God."

Above the whole scene stood a third angel with flaming sword crying, "Penance, penance, penance!" But the Virgin herself, radiating God's mercy, kept the consuming fire at bay.

Both Past and Future

Surely, we find here a frightening vision of what the twentieth century, still young when the apparitions took place, held in store for the Church. The infamous "November Revolution" in Russia, which occurred the very next month, gave birth to all the monstrous persecutions of Christians by Marxists throughout the world, ultimately killing many millions. The global spread of this political and spiritual poison had in fact been specifically predicted in an earlier portion of the Fatima message.

"If my requests are heeded," Our Lady had insisted, "Russia will be converted, and there will be peace; if not, she will spread her errors throughout the world, causing wars and persecutions of the Church. The good will be martyred; the Holy Father will have much to suffer; various nations will be annihilated."

As we've already seen, the Communist persecutions weren't the only anti-Christian horrors of the century: Believers suffered through the Nazi holocaust, Marxist revolutions in Mexico and Spain, genocide in Armenia and Rwanda ... and the list goes on. Just as the Congregation's commentary on the Fatima message observed, in Sr. Lucia's words, the twentieth-century "Church's path is thus described as a *via crucis* [way of the cross], as a journey through a time of violence, destruction and persecution.... In the vision we can recognize the last century as a century of martyrs, a century of suffering and persecution for the Church."

Persecution to Come?

Even so, the question remains: Does the twentieth-century nightmare represent the *whole* fulfillment of the vision of Fatima? Or does it point to terrors yet ahead as well?

Archbishop Tarcisio Bertone, the secretary of the Congregation for the Doctrine of the Faith, expressed his hope that the Holy Father's publication of the secret's final portion now "brings to an end a period of history marked by tragic human lust for power and evil." Yet he also warned: "If we have not yet seen the complete fulfillment of the final part of this prophecy, we are going toward it."

Will the twenty-first century bring a new dawn of peace for the Church? Or will it only prolong the diabolical darkness of the previous century? The ongoing agony of Catholics and other Christians in lands such as Sudan, Indonesia, China, Vietnam, and North Korea, and the growing hostility in nations such as India and Egypt, suggest that Fatima's prophecy may still be awaiting its total fulfillment.

Nor, we must conclude, are Christians in more "civilized" nations immune to the possibility of genuine persecution in the years to come. Germany, after all, boasted one of the most highly "civilized" cultures in the world when it gave birth to the Nazi obscenity. As a whole, contemporary Americans in particular seem so focused on material pursuits that they care little about whether religious and other civil liberties are being eroded, as long as the economic good times roll. If a new global Depression should happen to shatter our world, just as it shattered the Germans' world in the 1930s, our fragile system of government could give way, as theirs did, to a demonic demagogue.

Many Christians in the United States, Canada, and other traditionally open societies scoff at the notion that they might someday suffer anything beyond a few inconveniences for their faith. May God grant that they are right! Yet the current demonization of traditional Christians in the Western news and entertainment media and in educational settings has clear parallels to the demonization of Jewish people in pre-Nazi Germany.[2] Scoffers should remember that many German Jews on the very eve of the Holocaust also refused to believe that a massive, government-sponsored campaign of violence against them was on the horizon.

Pope John Paul II, who often peers into the future with remarkable insight, has in recent years called on Catholics to prepare themselves for such dangers. At the Jubilee celebration for priests, for example, he exhorted the clergy to struggle to offer "exemplary witness" to the faith, and to be ready for martyrdom if necessary. When he addressed the millions gathered at Rome for the Jubilee World Youth Day, he repeated that challenge—in words that echoed his messages to previous youth gatherings—saying that the faith may demand of young Catholics a "new martyrdom." "It is not by chance, dear young people," he reminded them, "that I wanted the witnesses to the faith in the twentieth century to be remembered at the Coliseum during this Holy Year."[3]

Was the pope speaking only to the Catholics from Africa and Asia? We dare not assume that he was, and we should prepare ourselves accordingly. To make ourselves ready for whatever the future may hold, we have much to learn from the martyrs who have gone before us and the martyrs who even now, this very day, in agonies largely ignored by the world, offer up their lives for the truth in imitation of their Lord.

Participation in His Passion

To learn the necessary lessons, we must recognize that the martyrs' stories not only repeat the pattern of Christ's passion; they complete it. This is not to say, of course, that Christ's sacrifice was anything less than perfect, nor did it lack anything necessary to redeem the world. Yet Scripture hints at a mystery in this regard. "Now I rejoice in my sufferings for your sake," wrote St. Paul to the Colossians, speaking as a man heading toward martyrdom. "And in my flesh I complete what is lacking in Christ's afflictions for the sake of his body, that is, the church" (Col 1:24).

Perhaps only God knows the full import of this text, but it certainly seems to suggest that the sufferings of Christ's followers stem from his, and are united with his, in such a way that they extend his grace to the Church in new ways. Through the life and death of the martyrs, the life and death of Christ himself is re-presented, made tangibly manifest to thousands of those who, from every nation and generation, had no opportunity to stand at the foot of the cross the day Jesus was executed.

At the very least, we can say that in a profound way the martyrs take part in Jesus' own pain. Because they are in Christ, their afflictions are truly his own. St. Peter told those who were facing persecution, "Rejoice in so far as you share Christ's sufferings" (1 Pt 4:13).

Completing the Picture

On perhaps a more practical level, the martyrs' stories can help to fill in what is lacking in our understanding of the Lord's passion. In a sense, the heroic tales of the martyrs are like later chapters of the gospel story, variations on the same plot. As we study their lives, the martyrs supply the details, so to speak, that are left out of the terse narratives offered by Matthew, Mark, Luke, and John.

The martyrs' stories thus often read like elaborations on the gospel accounts. In St. Justin's two apologies to the Church's imperial Roman persecutors, for example, we hear Christ answering through him Pilate's question, "What is truth?" In the complex personality of St. Thomas More's friend-turned-foe, King Henry VIII, we learn about the subtle intricacies of how the world comes to deceive itself and reject the truth.

In reading the penetrating, often introspective writings of St. Edith Stein, we come to appreciate more fully the costs of sacrificial suffering—not just physical, but psychological and spiritual as well. St. Flavian helps us work out the far-reaching implications of what loyalty to the truth may demand.

At the risk of sounding irreverent, we might even add that the martyrs uncover for us more fully the humor of Christ. In the Gospels, our Lord's wit flashes occasionally when he uses comic imagery to point out the slapstick absurdities of his opponents: hiding a flaming lamp under a bed of straw (see Mk 4:21); sending blind men out to lead one another into ditches (see Lk 6:39); sipping filth from polished goblets (see Mt 23:25-26); straining out gnats while swallowing camels (see Mt 23:24).

In the lives of the martyrs, such divine humor sometimes has the chance not just to flash but to shine a sustained beam of light into the darkness of a ludicrously fallen world. Blessed Miguel Pro's comic antics in disguise, like St. Thomas More's quips on the scaffold, show a godly contempt for even the worst of what the devil can do to a saint who's only a few steps away from heaven.

What Would Jesus Do?

The lives of the martyrs complete the picture of Jesus' life in other ways as well. Have you ever wondered how Jesus would have acted in specific circumstances that, given the particulars of the Incarnation, he never had to encounter? Perhaps you're facing some critical situation that would have been outside the experience of a Jewish man in first-century Palestine. Do you find yourself asking, "What would Jesus do?"

What, for example, would Jesus do as a young mother, nursing a newborn, who was arrested by government officials and told to choose between death or denying God? For at least the beginning of an answer to that question, reflect on the passion of St. Perpetua. What would Jesus do as a teenage hostage offered his freedom if he would submit to his captor's sexual advances? Think of St. Pelagius. How would Jesus spend his days in a Communist reeducation camp? Remember Marcel Van.

What would Jesus do? In short, surely much the same as what was done by those who later died for his sake. After all, the same Spirit of wisdom who filled Jesus also gave wisdom to the martyrs, allowing them to speak and act according to the will of his Father (see Mt 10:16-20; Lk 21:12-15).

We began this book by suggesting that in an effort to understand the martyrs we can look to the image of the suffering Christ for illumination. Yet the light actually shines in both directions. Meditation on the lives of the martyrs also brightens our understanding of the Crucified One. He is their precedent and pattern; they are, by participation in his glorious passion, his representation—the members of his body, broken, bleeding, and stretching out from his cross to heal the world.

The Help of the Martyrs

The martyrs' participation in Christ points toward a glorious reality that should give us great comfort: They serve us not only as role models, but as active channels of God's grace into our lives. Because of the communion of saints—the powerful solidarity and sharing of spiritual goods among those who are in Christ—Christians who have died for their faith and gone to their reward are able to share with us the benefits of that reward.

The Church discovered early on that God had granted the saints in heaven the ability to aid his people still on earth. In Revelation, for example, St. John shares with us his glimpse of the martyrs under the heavenly altar, praying that God will allow truth and justice to win out on the earth at last (see Rv 6:9-11). As we've seen, by the time one of St. John's disciples, St. Polycarp, met his death, the Christians of his flock already recognized that the martyr's relics were a valuable treasure to be preserved. Less than a century later, St. Cyprian of Carthage tells us, penitent Christians were lining up outside the prison cell doors of believers who were scheduled for execution, asking for promises of their intercession once they entered heaven.

Divine Favors

If there's one constant in the stories of the martyrs, throughout the world and down through the ages, it's the countless reports of miracles and other favors gained by their help after their death. Nor can we simply dismiss all these records as superstitious legends, for many of them have been left by trustworthy eyewitnesses and accompanied by medical documentation. St. Augustine, for example, reported numerous miracles in his day—some of which he witnessed himself—that were associated with martyrs' relics and obtained through their prayers. In his diocese of Hippo, so many miraculous healings occurred through the help of the martyrs that he finally gave instructions for them to be carefully documented.

How did the martyrs obtain such power? "For this faith they died," St. Augustine wrote, "and can now ask these benefits from the Lord in whose name they were slain.... By speaking the truth they suffered, and so won the power of working miracles."[4] In short, they work miracles because they are friends of God. They have become "partakers of the divine nature" (2 Pt 1:4), sharing in God's own power and authority.

To those who insist that the dead have no power to assist the living, St. Jerome replies: "If the Lamb is present everywhere, the same must be believed respecting those who are with the Lamb [see Rv 14:4]. And while the devil and the demons wander through the whole world, and with only too great speed present themselves everywhere, are martyrs—after the shedding of their blood—to be kept out of sight shut up in a coffin, from which they can't escape?... If apostles and martyrs while still in the body can pray for others, when they still have reason to be concerned for themselves, how much more must they do so when once they have won their crowns, overcome, and triumphed!"[5]

Spiritual Warfare

We'll probably never know just how much we owe to the martyrs' help until we ourselves, God willing, join them in heaven. Origen, a brilliant third-century theologian whose father was martyred and who himself suffered imprisonment and torture for his faith, speculated about a kind of spiritual warfare that he believed the martyrs undertake on our behalf.

"We are ... led to believe," he insisted, "that the powers of evil suffer defeat by the death of the holy martyrs; as if their patience, their confession even to death, and their zeal for piety blunted the edge of the onset of evil powers against them. In this way, the demons were dulled and exhausted, so that many others who had been conquered by them now raised their heads and were set free from the weight with which the evil powers had formerly oppressed and injured them."

St. Jerome went on to illustrate: Imagine that a brave man has caught and defanged a deadly snake that has been terrorizing a village. The people once intimidated can now be free because of his successful labors. In a similar way, the martyrs have helped to deliver us from evil by winning a battle against, and thus weakening, the ancient Serpent. "In some such way," St. Jerome concluded, "must we suppose the death of the most holy martyrs to operate, with many receiving benefit from it by an influence we cannot describe."[6]

Thus the martyrs aren't only the friends of God; they are our friends as well. They labor with God's own might on our behalf, and they eagerly await our requests for their aid.

Toward the Spring

We've noted that Pope John Paul II has repeatedly warned Catholics to be ready for martyrdom. Yet he's also predicted that "God is preparing a great springtime for Christianity."[7] Are these two visions of the future in conflict?

Not if we recall one last time Tertullian's maxim: *The blood of Christians is seed.* To speak of future martyrs is not to deny a great harvest for the Church. On the contrary, the one implies the other. Whether believers' blood will be spilled in Nairobi or New York, the fertile power of their testimony will blossom and bear eternal fruit.

Our task, then, is to make their witness our own. With them we must labor in prayer, in proclamation, in defense of truth and of truth's demands. We must reform our own lives to conform to Christ's life—for in the secret of Fatima, "Penance!" was the angel's stern cry over the ruins of our world.

In short, we must embrace the cross.

And what is the cross? It is "the imitation of Christ in faithful witness and patient and persevering work," says the Holy Father. "The cross is swimming against the tide, making decisions according to God's commandments despite misunderstanding, unpopularity, marginalization; the cross is the prophetic denunciation of injustice, of trampled freedoms, of violated rights; it is having to live where the Church is most opposed, obstructed and persecuted."[8]

At the foot of the cross, we may well live out our days persevering by grace under the adverse conditions John Paul has described. On the other hand, we may be called upon to lay down our lives. We may in fact be among those believers Sr. Lucia saw so vividly, so long ago, making their way up the mountain of the cross to kneel and to die.

If so, God's will be done. His grace will be sufficient. His cross will be our triumph. What higher calling could we have than to become the seed of heaven, lovingly scattered by God's hand to make possible the spring?

NOTES

INTRODUCTION
"The Blood of Christians Is Seed"

1. See Fr. Conrad Harkins, O.F.M., "On Franciscans, Archaeology, and Old Missions," in *Columbian Consequence*, ed. David Hurst Thomas (Washington, D.C.: Smithsonian Institute, 1990), 459–72; Harkins, "The Georgia Martyrs (1597)," *Franciscan Way*, Winter 1997, 16.
2. "Thousands Flock to Funeral of Priest Murdered in Kenya," Catholic World News Service, August 30, 2000; (www.CWNews.com).
3. Pope John Paul II, *Crossing the Threshold of Hope*, ed. Vittorio Messori, trans. Jenny McPhee and Martha McPhee (New York: Alfred E. Knopf, 1994), 177.
4. For more on this matter, see Michael Freze, S.F.O., *The Making of Saints* (Huntington, Ind.: Our Sunday Visitor, 1991).

ONE
"An Image of His Master"

1. These items were gleaned from the July 2000 issue of *The Catholic World Report*, the August 27–September 2 edition of *The National Catholic Register*, online reports of the

Zenit News Agency (www.zenit.org), and news stories gathered at the website of the Eternal Word Television Network (www.ewtn.com). For additional documentation, see the Annual Reports to Congress on International Religious Freedom (www.state.gov/www/global/human_rights/irf/irf_rpt/index.html).

2. Robert Royal, *Catholic Martyrs of the Twentieth Century: A Comprehensive World History* (New York: Crossroad, 2000), 31, 34.
3. See "Pro-Abortion Violence in the U.S. and Canada Includes 55 Murders, Report Claims," *National Catholic Register,* August 27–September 2, 2000, 5.
4. Quoted in Greg Burke, "The Church's Newest Martyrs," *Columbia,* July 2000, 5.
5. Pope John Paul II, *Tertio Millennio Adveniente* (November 14, 1994), IV, 37; emphasis in the original.
6. John Paul II, *Tertio,* IV, 37, emphasis in the original.
7. The Second Vatican Council, *Lumen Gentium,* V, 42.
8. *Catechism of the Catholic Church,* par. 2472.
9. *Catechism,* par. 2473, 2474.

TWO
"Crying in the Wilderness"

1. This chapter is based on the Gospel texts that provide us somewhat piecemeal information about the Baptist's life: Jn 1:6-8, 15, 19-40; 3:23-36; 4:1; 5:33-36; 10:40-42; Mt 3:1-17; 4:12; 9:14-17; 11:2-19; 14:1-13; 16:14; 17:10-13; 21:25-27, 32; and parallel passages in Mark and Luke. Since ancient times Christians have debated how best to

harmonize the details of these varying accounts; any attempt to do so, such as the present one, necessarily involves a degree of speculation. In order to focus on and illuminate the implications of St. John's martyrdom, I have taken further liberties in speculating about certain aspects of the drama about which the Gospels are silent.

THREE
"The Cup That I Drink, You Will Drink"

1. The rest of this chapter follows the scriptural account in Acts, beginning with the second chapter. A few additional details have been supplied, as noted, from the more trustworthy ancient traditions.
2. St. Ambrose, *Exposition of the Christian Faith*, 3, 17, 137.
3. St. John Chrysostom, Homily 66, 6.
4. Tertullian, *Apology*, 5.

FOUR
"We Must Obey God Rather Than Men"

1. Tertullian, *Apology*, 40.
2. For the complete eyewitness account, see "The Encyclical Epistle of the Church at Smyrna Concerning the Martyrdom of the Holy Polycarp," in *The Ante-Nicene Fathers: Translations of the Writings of the Fathers Down to A.D. 325*, Alexander Roberts and James Donaldson, eds. (Grand Rapids: Eerdmans, 1987, American reprint of the Edinburgh edition), I, 37–44.
3. For the complete story, composed mostly of St. Perpetua's

prison journal, see "The Martyrdom of Perpetua and Felicitas," R. E. Wallis, trans., in *Ante-Nicene Fathers*, III, 697–706.

4. Given these circumstances, it's difficult to understand how some contemporary scholars of this historical period claim that the Christians under Muslim rule weren't "persecuted," and consider the Cordoban martyrs unreasonable extremists for challenging the status quo. Such a claim is simply absurd. Both Christians and Muslims who wanted to be Christians were banned, on pain of death, from exercising the most basic human rights to freedom of religion and freedom of speech, to say nothing of the unjust taxes and other oppressive laws they endured.

5. The primary sources for the story of the martyrs of Cordoba are Eulogius' letters and his *Documentum martyriale*, *Liber apologeticus martyrum*, and *Memoriale sanctorum*, as well as the *Indiculus luminosus* and *Vita Eulogii* written by his friend Paulus Alvarus.

6. This poem, "The Passion of St. Pelagius," is our primary source of information about the young martyr.

FIVE

"The Overthrower of Our Gods"

1. The primary sources for the story of St. Justin's life are his *First Apology, Second Apology, Dialogue With Trypho the Jew*, and *The Martyrdom of the Holy Martyrs Justin...*; see *Ante-Nicene Fathers*, I, 150–270, 305–6.

2. St. Justin's comment reflects his confidence that, if he resisted the torments and remained faithful to death, he would have his reward. From the earliest periods of

Church history, it was believed that those who endured martyrdom for Christ went right away to heaven, assured both of salvation and immediate glorification (without the need for substantial time in purgatory). This conviction was reflected in the fact that in the early centuries, authentic Christian martyrs were automatically acclaimed as saints.

3. The primary sources for the life of St. Boniface are his epistles and Willibald's *Life of Boniface;* see C.H. Talbot, *The Anglo-Saxon Missionaries in Germany* (New York: Sheed and Ward, 1954). For a fine essay on the saint, see Christopher Dawson, "St. Boniface," in *Saints and Ourselves,* Philip Caraman, S.J., ed. (Garden City, N.Y.: Image Books, 1958), 77–84.

4. Christianity came early to the great cities of northern Africa and to Ethiopia as well, but the remainder of the continent remained isolated from the gospel for many centuries.

5. For more on Blessed Michael Nakashima, the other martyrs of Japan, St. Isaac Jogues and the martyrs of North America, and a number of other Jesuit martyrs, see Joseph N. Tylenda, S.J., *Jesuit Saints and Martyrs: Short Biographies of the Saints, Blesseds, Venerables and the Servants of God of the Society of Jesus,* 2d ed. (Chicago: Loyola Press, 1998).

6. Tylenda, 453.

7. Tylenda, 453.

8. Detailed information about the lives of the martyrs of North America can be found in their careful reports to their superiors in France; see R.G. Thwaites, ed., *Jesuit Relations and Allied Documents* (Cleveland: Burrows Brothers, 1896–1901). The martyrs of North America were canonized by Pope Pius XI in 1930.

9. Jean de Brébeuf, in Thwaites, X, 89.

10. Pierre Baird, quoted in D.B. Quinn, *New American World* (New York: Arno Press and Hector Bye, 1979), 4:392-94.

11. Tylenda, 352.

12. For more on the martyrs of Uganda, see Ann Ball, *Modern Saints: Their Lives and Faces, Book I* (Rockford, Ill.: TAN, 1983), 86–94; J.F. Faupel, *African Holocaust* (New York: P.J. Kenedy, 1962); and Francis Marion, *New African Saints* (Milan, Italy: Ancora, 1964). In all, twenty-two martyrs were canonized by Pope Paul VI as the Martyrs of Uganda in 1964.

SIX
"My Greatest Enemies, My Best Friends"

1. Pope John Paul II, Address to the Jubilee Ecumenical Commemoration of Twentieth-Century Martyrs, May 7, 2000; quoted in "Blood of Christ's Witnesses Gives Impulse to Ecumenism," Zenit News Agency website, May 7, 2000, (www.zenit.org).

2. For more on St. Flavian (and many other Catholic martyrs), see Alban Butler, *The Lives of the Fathers, Martyrs and Other Principal Saints* (London: Sadlier, 1864), 2:143.

3. The sources for the life of St. Thomas are numerous, including the seven thick volumes entitled *Materials for the History of Thomas Becket, Archbishop of Canterbury*, James Craigie Robertson, ed. (London: Master of the Rolls, 1875ff). For a fine short essay, see Leslie Macfarlane, "St. Thomas of Canterbury," in Caraman, 85–100.

4. St. Thomas More's first biography remains in many ways the most fascinating; see William Roper, *The Lyfe of Sir Thomas More, Knighte,* Elsie Vaughn Hitchcock, ed. (London: E.E.T.S., 1935). Other biographies abound.

5. For excerpts from St. Thomas More's extensive works, and more about his irrepressible sense of humor, see *Be Merry in God: 60 Reflections From the Writings of St. Thomas More,* Paul Thigpen, comp. (Ann Arbor, Mich.: Servant, 1999).

6. For more on St. Andrew Bobola, see Tylenda, 136-38; John J. Rohr, S.J. "Witness Unto Death," *The Catholic Hearth,* May 1998, 11–14.

7. Rohr, 13.

SEVEN

"Long Live Christ the King!"

1. Pope John Paul II, World Youth Day Homily, August 19, 2000; quoted in "Holy Father Calls Youth to a 'New Martyrdom,'" *National Catholic Register* 76, no. 35 (August 27–September 2, 2000), 7.

2. Quoted in Francis Clement Kelley, *Blood-Drenched Altars: A Catholic Commentary on the History of Mexico* (Milwaukee, Wis.: Bruce, 1935), 342–43.

3. For a full account of Blessed Miguel Pro's life, see Gerald F. Muller, C.S.C., *With Life and Laughter: The Life of Father Pro* (Boston: Pauline, 1996); Ann Ball, *Blessed Miguel Pro: Twentieth-Century Martyr* (Rockford, Ill.: Tan, 1996).

4. Muller, 32.

5. Quoted in Muller, 106–7.

6. Ball, *Blessed Miguel*, 169.
7. Quoted in Ball, *Modern Saints*, 302.
8. Ball, *Modern Saints*, 302.
9. Ball, *Blessed Miguel*, xi.
10. Fr. Pro was beatified by Pope John Paul II on September 25, 1988.
11. H.R. Trevor-Roper, ed., *Hitler's Secret Conversations, 1941–44* (New York: Octagon, 1976), 247.
12. Space won't allow here for a critique of recent slanders against Pius XII as "Hitler's pope." Yet a number of published sources already provide all the primary documentation and careful analysis necessary to undermine utterly any absurd claims that the Vatican or the German Catholic clergy as a whole were Nazi sympathizers or collaborators. For a careful and thorough debunking of the new "myth" of "Hitler's pope," see Ronald J. Rychlak, *Hitler, the War and the Pope* (Huntington, Ind.: Our Sunday Visitor, 2000).
13. For a full account of St. Edith Stein's life, see Waltraud Herbstrith, *Edith Stein: A Biography*, trans. Bernard Bonowitz, O.C.S.C (New York: Harper & Row, 1985); Hilda Graef, *The Scholar and the Cross: The Life and Work of Edith Stein* (London: Longman, Green, 1955).
14. Quoted in Graef, 10.
15. Herbstrith, 20.
16. Herbstrith, 25.
17. Herbstrith, 53.
18. Herbstrith, 53.
19. Graef, 112.
20. Graef, 141.
21. Graef, 184.
22. Graef, 188.

23. Herbstrith, 95.

24. Critics of Pope Pius XII's reticence (it was never silence) at
times about publicly condemning Nazi atrocities must consider this incident as well as others before presuming to
judge his motivations or wisdom. He had clear and tragic
evidence that public denunciations would lead to immediate reprisals, including murders. Is it any wonder that he
often chose to oppose the Nazis behind the scenes instead?

25. Edith Stein, "The Prayer of the Church," in *The Writings
of Edith Stein*, Hilda Graef, ed. (London: Peter Owen,
Ltd., 1956), 40.

26. St. Edith Stein was canonized by Pope John Paul II on
October 11, 1998. Some have objected to her canonization as a martyr, claiming she was put to death by Nazis as
a Jew rather than as a Catholic. But the reality is more
complicated. The wave of arrests that resulted in her being
sent to the camp and murdered was directed specifically at
Catholics of Jewish background, in retribution for a condemnation of Nazi atrocities by the *Catholic* clergy. This
suggests that in her particular case the murderers were
motivated by revenge against the Church, as well as by
hatred for Jews. In addition, St. Edith herself had asked
God for the privilege of offering her life for Christ, and
whatever her tormentors' motives, it was apparently clear
in her mind that she wished to die as a martyr for the
Church as well as for the Jewish people.

27. Statistics from Didier Rance, *Catholiques d'Ukraine, des
catacombes ... a la lumiere* (Paris: Bibliotheque AED,
1992), 13, cited in Royal, 69.

28. For a full account of Van's life, see Fr. Marie-Michel, *Love
Cannot Die: A Life of Marcel Van* (Montpelier: Librairie
Artheme Fayard, 1990).

29. Marie-Michel, 116.

30. Marie-Michel, 172.

31. Marie-Michel, 175.

32. Marie-Michel, 234. The cause for the beatification of Servant of God Marcel Van was introduced March 26, 1997.

EIGHT
"In Persecution the Church Begins and Ends"

1. The Congregation for the Doctrine of the Faith, at the Holy Father's directive, published the entire secret, including all three parts, along with commentary. The whole set of documents appears, among other places, at the website of the Eternal Word Television Network, (www.ewtn.com). The following quotes come from these texts.

2. For a thorough analysis of this development in Germany, see George L. Mosse, *The Crisis of German Ideology: Intellectual Origins of the Third Reich* (New York: Grosset and Dunlap, 1964).

3. Quoted in "Birthday and Jubilee: Priests Join Pope for Celebration," *Catholic World Report*, July 2000, 6; Raymond De Souza, "Millions Flock to Rome With Pope," *National Catholic Register*, August 27–September 2, 2000, 7.

4. St. Augustine, *City of God*, XXII, 8–10; quote is from 9 and 10.

5. St. Jerome, *Against Vigilantius*, 5.

6. Origen, *Commentary on John*, 6, 36.

7. Pope John Paul II, *Lumen Gentium*, 15.

8. Pope John Paul II, Message for World Mission Sunday, May 28, 1996.